TRAMS
&
TROLLEYBUSES
in
ILFORD

*

L.A.THOMSON

*

1979

THE OPENING TRAM CAR, ILFORD LANE, MAY 27th, 1903.

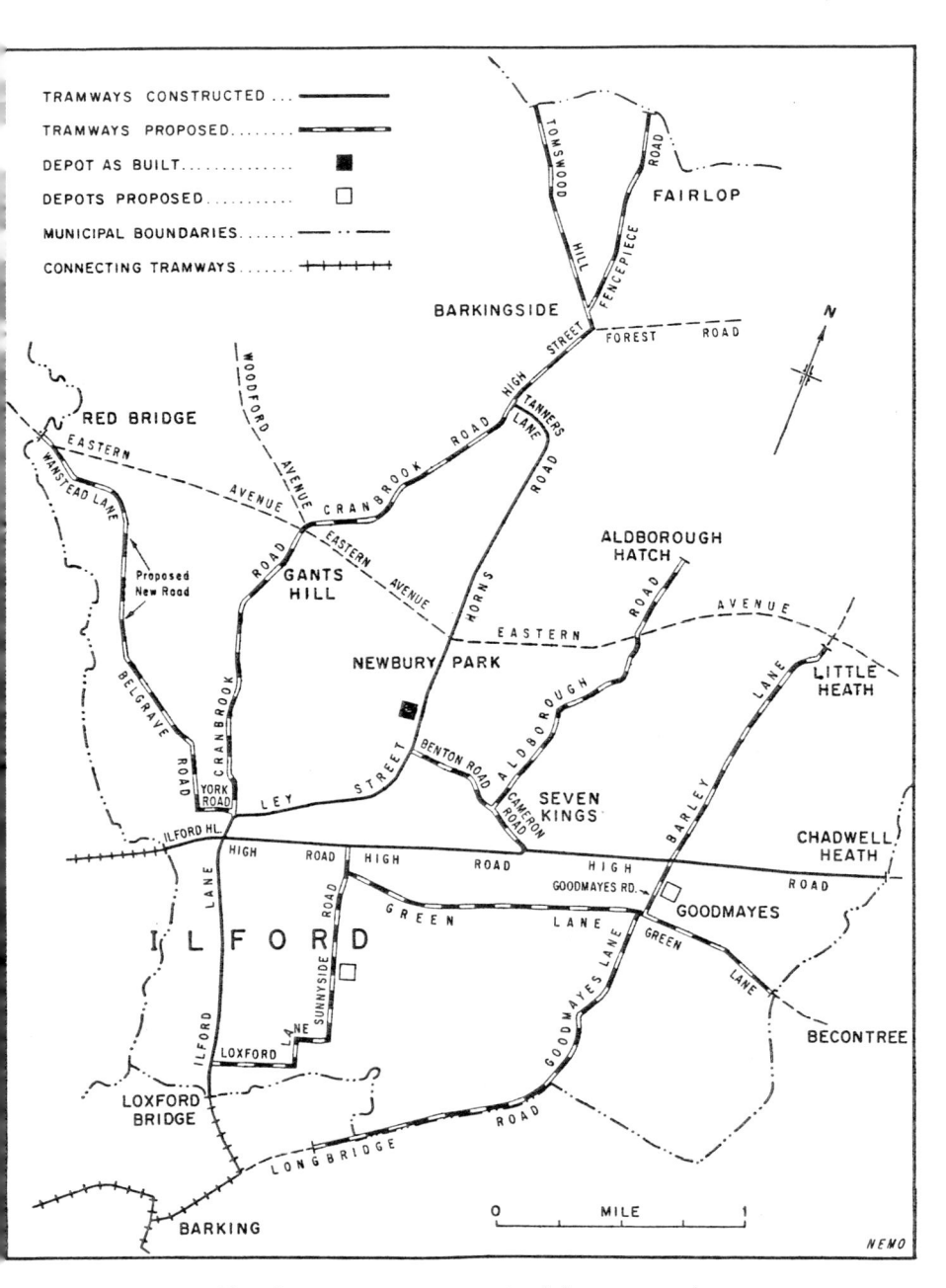

Map of tram routes constructed and those proposed

CONTENTS

Introduction	5
The beginning	7
The system settles down	19
The Great War	29
The twenties	32
The thirties	39
London Transport	45
Trolleybuses	49
Technical Data	52

Published by THE ILFORD & DISTRICT HISTORICAL SOCIETY.
Hon. Secretary: P.J. Wright, 174 Aldborough Road South, Ilford, Essex.

Researched and written by Leonard A. Thomson.

© L.A. Thomson. 1979.

Printed by Nemo Productions, Hartley, Dartford, Kent.

TRAMS AND TROLLEYBUSES IN ILFORD

INTRODUCTION

There were never any horse-drawn trams in Ilford, the nearest being at Manor Park, (having come from Stratford), which were operated by the North Metropolitan Tramways Company, who had depot premises at No. 512, Romford Road, Manor Park. In a way, this was fortunate for the local council, bacause Local Authorities could exercise their rights (under the Tramways Act of 1870) to purchase the lines in their areas when the period of tenure had elapsed. Even then however, the negotiations for transfer could be lengthy. So Ilford started with electric cars.

At the other end of the district, in Chadwell Heath, several schemes were put forward to extend the line as built, to Romford and Gidea Park. The first, in 1902, was promoted by the Romford Council. Other promotions, up to 1908, were made by various tramway companies, including the Metropolitan Electric Tramway Company, which, at that time, was operating trams in north London.

Chadwell Heath also featured in further proposals in the 1920s, when a line was mooted from Barking Station to Chadwell Heath, via the enormous LCC estate at Becontree.

My acquaintance with the Ilford trams came late in the 1914/18 war, when I was but a child. My family lived in Ley Street, and trams passed by every few minutes, a few hundred yards away from Ilford Broadway, where cars belonging to East Ham, and West Ham Corporations, as well as those of the LCC could be seen.

In those far-off days, working hours were longer, and the week-end relaxation seemed very attractive. The crowd movement on a Saturday afternoon to the local football ground was fascinating to observe; and many people would take the tram on a Sunday to journey to Barkingside, as a starting-off point for rambles to Hainault Forest and beyond.

The tramways did not have a long span of life, but played a large part in the development of the district, and in the day-to-day needs of the people. On a summer's day, to alight at the "Horns", and walk across the fields to Victoria Road, accompanied by the song of the skylark, was a stroll of sheer delight, which I still remember.

Today, the fields have gone; the trams have gone; and the lark is seldom heard in these parts.

In conclusion, may I thank the many people who have been so helpful on this project:- the Library Staffs at :-

>Redbridge Reference Library;
>The Patent Office;
>The British Museum;
>The House of Lords Record Office; and
>The Local Press.

In particular, I offer my thanks for much information to Mr. Ernest Blake of Newbury Park, who worked at the Ilford Depot; and to Richard Elliott, a friend of many years standing, and one-time Technical Assistant with London Transport, and to Mr. Jim North, C. Eng., F.I.CHEM.E., M.INST.F., who assisted with the initial typing of the script.

To everyone who contributed, no matter how small, my sincere "Thanks".

May 1975.
Updated for publication, January 1979.

*

No. **10**

ILFORD URBAN DISTRICT COUNCIL.

DINNER

AT THE "ANGEL HOTEL," ILFORD,

On Saturday, March 14th, 1903,

At 6 p.m., sharp.

TO CELEBRATE THE OPENING OF THE ILFORD ELECTRIC TRAMWAYS.

GEORGE W. M. GOTT, Esq., J.P.,
Chairman of the Council, Presiding.

TICKET 5/-

JOHN W. BENTON,
Clerk to the Council.

THE BEGINNING

The end of the 19th century saw many enormous housing projects come to fruition in the Ilford area, mainly through the efforts of A. Cameron Corbett, Esq., and, to administer to the needs of some forty thousand people resident, the Ilford Urban District Council was created in 1894. Many of the residents were employed in London, and a local transport system to feed the railway stations became a necessity. In September 1898, the Council appointed Mr. W.C.C. Hawtayne, MIEE, (at a fee of 4% of the contract value) as Consulting Engineer of the electric tramway which the Council proposed to construct. Messrs. Baker, Lees & Company were the Parliamentary Agents; a Provisional Order was granted on 25th April 1899, and, on the 2nd May a Bill of Confirmation was introduced to the House of Lords and read for the first time.

Meanwhile, a deputation from the Council visited Glasgow, Bradford, Blackpool, Leeds and Kidderminster, to see the systems at work in these places and, on their return, it was agreed that the overhead system of power transmission was the cheapest and the most suitable for Ilford, and the 3'-6" gauge was selected for the track work. By then, the neighbouring East Ham Council had begun constructing their tramway, having the standard gauge of 4'-$8\frac{1}{2}$". Wisely, Ilford Council applied to Parliament for an alteration to its Bill, so as to coincide with this gauge, and confirmation came through on 22nd May 1900.

A depot site was selected in Ley Street, at the junction with Perth Road, covering $2\frac{1}{2}$ acres, and a loan of £4,400 was raised to develop the building. Next door was the Electricity Works, which had a brick chimney shaft 180 feet high. Half the cost of the power station was borne by the tramway. To the north, was the Council Works Depot of $4\frac{1}{2}$ acres, where a well was sunk, the cost being equally shared between the Works, the Tramway, and the Electricity Department. The foundation stone of the Depot was laid on the 25th August 1900, by Councillor Henry Weedon.

The tramway routes applied for in the 1898 Act were:-

No. 1: From Aldersbrook boundary (Ilford Hill), to Chadwell Heath boundary, at Station Road:
Distance: 3 miles 00.80 chains.
No. 2: From junction with No.1 at Goodmayes, via Goodmayes Road and Stoop Lane (now Goodmayes Lane) to Wood Lane:
Distance: 1 mile 06-00 chains.
No. 3: From junction with No.2 at Wood Lane, via Longbridge Road, past Faircross, to a point where Hurstbourne Gardens is now situated:
Distance: 1 mile*

* The Act gives the measurement as 1 mile 09.15 chains, but this appears to be in error.

No. 4: An East-to-South junction at Barley Lane, Goodmayes:
Distance: 1.70 chains.
No. 5: An East-to-North junction at Barley Lane, Goodmayes:
Distance: 2.20 chains.
No. 6: From Goodmayes via Barley Lane to Little Heath (the "Haw Bush").
Distance: 1 mile 0.70 chains.
No. 7: Ilford Broadway to Roman Road:
Distance: 76.50 chains.
No. 7a: The eastern track from Roman Road to Loxford Bridge:
Distance: 8.50 chains.
(The western side of Ilford Lane, between these points was in Barking, the boundary being in the middle of the road. The Essex County Council however, expressed its opinion that all tracks should be double, and lent their assistance to widen Ilford Lane between Rutland Road and Loxford Bridge, to accommodate the two tracks).
No. 8: An East-to-South junction at Ilford Broadway:
Distance: 1.25 chains.
No. 9: A West-to-North junction at Ilford Broadway:
Distance: 6.00 chains.
No. 10: A North-to-East junction at Ilford Broadway:
Distance 1.55 chains.
No. 11: From Ilford Station to "The Chequers", Barkingside, via Cranbrook Road:
Distance: 2 miles 29.50 chains.
No. 12: From Ilford Station to "The Chequers", Barkingside, via Ley St:
Distance: 2 miles 38.90 chains.
No. 13: An East-to-North junction at Ley Street/Cranbrook Road:
Distance: 1.50 chains.
No. 14: From "The Chequers" Barkingside, to Chigwell boundary on Tomswood Hill:
Distance: 1 mile 27.70 chains.
No. 15: From Fencepiece Road/Tomswood Hill junction to the Chigwell boundary at Fencepiece Road:
Distance: 65.90 chains.

Of these, only Nos: 1, 7, 7a, 8, 9, 10 and 12, were built. A simple ceremony took place on 6th March 1902, when councillor Ben Bailey, Chairman of the Tramways Committee, assisted by his Vice-Chairman, Councillor A. Wilde, fixed a rivet that held a bonding strap to the track.

The poles which had been planted in the centre of the High Road from Cleveland Road to the "Seven Kings Hotel", from which the overhead wires were suspended were soon seen as a menace and a danger to other road users, but it was not until 1912 that any attempt was made to replace them. In those days the traction poles were painted with a dark-green base, and light-green upper works. Many citizens voiced their opinions on the vexed question of the centre poles, even before the trams started running. One brave soul put pen to paper, and wrote these following lines :-

8

"When the centre poles were settled, the fun, we fear, was ended,
But the coronating farce brought us more than was intended.
Then the censure on the School Board, made us nearly split our sides:
Now another squabble's started, all about our tramway rides.
Our Council "is a hot 'un", 'tis their pride they know it well,
They'll bust up all creation; they're at it now pell-mell.
Lay down the trams, they'll pay the rates; go at it like a blizzard,
There's something in our past, that sticks in the public gizzard".

Meanwhile, construction continued, and on 11th July 1902, the Chadwell Heath line was reported as almost complete; and 29th August saw the Barkingside line finished. Ilford Broadway, with rails going in all directions (except north-to-south), had corresponding overhead cables in such fine array, that the locals lost no time in re-naming the Broadway "Cobweb Corner".

Many members of the Tramways Committee visited Brighton, Southampton, Portsmouth and Croydon, all places where tramways were already in operation, in order to get acquainted with an undertaking which they were now called upon to control.

A Provisional Order was applied for to cover the following extensions :-

No. 1:   4 furlongs 7.0 chains along Cranbrook Road to a terminus near Beaufort Gardens;
No. 1a: 1.5 chains double track North-to-East junction from Cranbrook Road into Ley Street;
No. 2:   Double track in Hainault Street;
No. 2a: North-to-West junction into the High Road:
No. 2b.   South-to-West junction, Hainault Street into Ley Street;

The application was made on 24th October 1902, and withdrawn on the 13th February 1903, because of dissent by many of the Cranbrook Road frontagers.

Hainault Street featured in a previous proposal, along with Green Lanes, and Goodmayes Road to the High Road. Further lines were suggested from Ilford Station, via Cranbrook Road and the Drive to "The Red House"; from the Wash in the Cranbrook Road to Barkingside, either Fulwell Hatch, Claybury Hospital Gates, or "The Maypole". However, no application was made. Another suggestion about this time was for a standard gauge railway to leave the new Woodford line near Benton Road bridge, to convey coals to the Electricity Generating Station in Ley Street. At that time, all these parts were in open country.

A report of 28th December 1902 stated that seven cars had been delivered, and on Saturday 10th January 1903, a trial run was made over the lines that were completed. It would appear that two men from the British Thomson-Houston Company (BTH) arrived at the Depot to test the motors and other electrical equipment made by them, only to find that no trolley poles had been delivered. Without these parts, the tramcars were immobilised. A telegram was despatched to the works, and a trolley arrived at 7.30 am., on 10th January. This was fitted to a car, which then set out for Barkingside, with Councillors Gott, Bailey, Weston and Deveson on board, together with A.H. Shaw (Council Electrical Engineer), and G.R. Spurr, the Tramways Manager.

During track construction at one point, the concrete bed was laid across a gas main. The Gas Company were successful in obtaining a Court Order requiring the Tramway Department to remove the concrete, which prompted the local poet into verse once more :-

> "This is the thing to clear us, rough shod the high horse ride,
> Haste, haste, now good Contractors, in you our trust we bide,
> The work was done, the tramway built, the rails and ducts laid down,
> And the cars were forthwith ordered, to be despatched from town.
> Alas, those hopes were blighted, for in spite of all their pains
> They's stopped the Gas Works business, by covering their mains.
> The Company made objection; the Council soon found out,
> That the mains must be uncovered; that's what the row's about".

As much of the work had now been completed, some of the citizens were expressing concern on the non-appearance of the tramcars. In a lighter vein, a letter to the Press suggested that Councillor Ben Bailey should serenade the cars in the Depot, using these words to the music of a popular song :-

> "Come out this happy morn,
> All in a row, all in a row,
> They came gliding down Ley Street
> Rather a startling sight to meet,
> For we've been promised them
> Long long ago,
> Nineteen jolly old cars, all in a row".

After rendering this ditty, it was suggested that the Depot doors would open, and the cars emerge, the writer considering that this could better be done at 1 am. The ghostly procession would then proceed to the Broadway, where Mr. W.P.Griggs would be noted guarding his Clock Tower against any acts of hooligans. From here, Councillor Ben Bailey would lead the procession to the Town Hall, carrying a red flag, followed by six cream-coloured ponies drawing a decorated tar boiler. Refreshments would be served, the Councillors would then emerge (after slapping a few pence on the rates), and the tramcars would be despatched to their various destinations (except Ilford Lane). "It would be noted that Ben Bailey was wearing blinkers, thus confirming the forward-looking policy of the Council, whose members are steadfast in their duties. Come what may, our elected representatives have a great future behind them".

The sweeper car was now making trips over the system. In fact, its revolving broom caught fire, the flames being extinguished with buckets of water. A Contractor's Test Run was made at midnight on the 12th February 1903. These test runs created a lot of interest, and, it appears, a lot of passengers, for the Council decided that no further runs were to be made without their being informed, and they, in turn, would invite the press. (At this time, the "Ilford Recorder" was not on the phone, and this connection was made through the good offices of their next door neighbour).

Mr.R.McKelvey was appointed Car Shed Foreman, (at £2.10.0 per week); Mr.W.H.White was Chief Inspector at £2.0.0. per week. Inspectors Collins and Mears were paid £1.15.0. per week.

Car No.7 crosses Ilford Station Bridge.

(Croucher & Howard)

Hurst Nelson bogie car No.13 at the depot in 1903, seen in original condition.

Domed-roof car No.29, also West Ham car No.61 seen at Ilford Broadway.

(Hornby Picture)

Motormen were paid 6¼d per hour; conductors 5¾d per hour. A checking Clerk received £80 per year, two cash clerks were paid £1.0.0. per week, and a junior clerk received £30 per year.

The Depot in Ley Street became a centre of interest, as much testing of cars and equipment was carried on inside and could be seen by passers-by. As the system neared completion, the Board of Trade was notified, and the official inspection arranged for the 6th March. At 10 am., Col. Von Donop dealt with the permanent way, and Alexander Trotter the overhead cables. The car left the Depot for the Broadway, thence travelled to Chadwell Heath, and then back to the Broadway and on to Barkingside, where it was found that the rail was too close to the kerb outside Dr. Barnardo's Village Church.

The Council undertook to attend to it immediately, and the car then proceeded back to the Broadway, where the Inspectors joined their train back to town, and the councillors and other officials retired to "The Angel", it being understood that each man should pay for his own refreshment.

A large party gathered at the Depot on the afternoon of Saturday 14th March 1903, when Councillor Ben Bailey addressed the Drivers and Conductors:-

"First of all, I want you, Motormen, to have clear heads, keen eyes, and steady hands, always thinking of your work, not driving recklessly.

I want to remind the Conductors that a civil tongue goes a long way, and if ever you have passengers who attempt to kick over the traces, it is far better to use civil words than force".

The passengers now climbed aboard. Car No.1 contained the councillors and their wives. Car No.2 contained members of the School Board and the Press. Cars 3 and 4 conveyed various other officials, their wives, and the contractors.

Car No.1 moved off, driven by Councillor Gott, Chairman of the Council. No.2 was driven by Councillor Ben Bailey, Chairman of the Tramways Committee, and No.3 by Councillor Weston, Vice-Chairman of the Tramways Committee. However, the sun disappeared behind a cloud bank, and the storm broke with a deluge of rain which broke up the procession. The cars travelled from the Depot to Ilford Broadway, thence to Chadwell Heath, and then back to the Town Hall, where the passengers alighted, and heard Councillor Gott declare the system open to fare-paying passengers and that there were 14 cars available for service as from that day. Councillor Ben Bailey was also called upon to speak, but he was continually heckled by a man who kept calling out, "Don't you know me?" to which the worthy Councillor replied "In the ordinary way, I probably do, but as you are disguised by beer, I find it difficult". To shouts of "Never mind him" he continued, and finished by saying "May Ilford prosper; may the electric light scheme prosper; and may all those fanatics be turned out of the town". (Loud cheers and laughter).

The councillors and their wives dined at "The Angel" that night. As so many of the townsfolk were drinking and toasting the undertaking at about the same time, it is doubtful whether the question was ever raised as to who was footing the councillors' bill.

The lengths of the routes were as follows :-

Ilford Hill	to Green Lane	1400 yards
Green Lane	to Seven Kings Stat	1285 yards
Seven Kings	to Barley Lane	1055 yards
Barley Lane	to Chadwell Heath	1560 yards

Total: 3 miles 20 yards.

| Ilford Broadway to Hampton Road: | 940 yards |
| Hampton Road to Loxford Bridge: | 928 yards |

Total: 1 mile 108 yards.

Ilford Station	to Sams Green ("The Bell"):	1155 yards
Sams Green	to Hatch Lane ("Greengate"):	1155 yards
Hatch Lane	to Buntingbridge Farm:	1110 yards
Buntingbridge Fm.	to Barkingside Terminus:	960 yards

Total: 2 miles 860 yards.

The first cars were from the Broadway to Chadwell Heath at 5 am; to Barkingside at 5.30 am. The last cars were at 11.05 pm, and 11.15 pm on Saturdays. On Sundays, the first cars left the Broadway at 10 am; and the last car left the Broadway at 10.05 pm for Chadwell Heath and for Barkingside.

The undertaking was not without its teething troubles. In the first few weeks, Car No.7 collided with a steamroller, and Car No.1 had its trolley de-wired in Ilford Lane, the head getting caught under a bracket arm, wrenching the trolley mast from the floor of the top deck.

The stormy weather that prevailed about this time was attributed to spots on the sun. One Councillor was heard to remark, "Had we opened the Ilford Lane line at the same time as the rest, no doubt the sun would have disintegrated".

The department made enquiries whether the room below the Clock Tower could be used as a paying-in kiosk, but it was decided that this was impractical, and negotiations were opened with the Great Eastern Railway for the use of a site in the station yard, on which to place a hut. Takings on the first few days of the running of the cars were :-

Saturday	March 14th:	£ 55.10. 4.
Sunday		£131.15.10.
Monday		£ 57.12. 4½.
Tuesday		£ 52.14. 9.
Wednesday		£ 44. 6. 7.

Advertising on the cars was an additional source of revenue, and an arrangement was made with Mr. A. E. Abrahams, an agent, who paid the Council £31.10. 0. per annum per car, for this privelege. A further £2.10. 0. per annum per car was paid in respect of six cars that carried a side advertisement for the Borough Theatre, Stratford, which allowed a paper insert to be attached weekly, giving details of the current productions. One councillor voiced his disapproval of the beautiful cars being adorned with advertisements, but was informed that the revenue paid the insurance, and left cash to spare.

During the first quarter ending June 13th, advertising revenue amounted to £145.10.0; fares taken were £5,679.2.5½. Expenditure accounted for £4,629.11.10; leaving a profit of £1,204.0.5½. Abnormal loads were dealt with at weekends, and an order was given to conductors not to give change for halfpenny fares on Saturdays and Sundays.

For the first week of operating the fares collected totalled £404.3.5., the miles run by the cars was 7,802, and hence takings per car-mile amounted to 12.43d. Units of electricity consumed totalled 8,207, working out at 1.05d. per mile.

Electricity was supplied by the Council's Power Station, located alongside the tram depot in Ley Street. Power was supplied at a pressure of 500 volts, the station being equipped with five steam-driven generators having a total output of 1,600 Kw. In an emergency, this could be increased to 1,925 Kw. Four water-tube boilers provided the steam for the generators.

As the system settled down, certain alterations were made. Following complaints, the "Request Stop" at Seven Kings Brook was made compulsory. Workmens Tickets were issued from 5 am. to 7 am. for return by any car after 1 pm, or 12 noon on Saturdays.

Of the 18 cars in stock, 10 were required for the Chadwell Heath run, and 4 for that to Barkingside, leaving 4 in the Depot for repairs. In order to increase the service, a further 4 cars were ordered on 10th April 1903 from Messrs. Hurst Nelson, of Motherwell. These were 4-wheelers, similar to the original twelve, and costing £500 each. A promise was given for delivery of the cars by July 7th. Due to the urgency, a Councillor suggested a late delivery Penalty Clause be inserted in the contract at £10 per car per week. However, it was pointed out that the Council might be called upon to pay £10 per car for cars delivered before the due date, which raised the question as to whether the Public Auditor would sanction such payment, and not surcharge the Councillors.

Shortly after the trams began operating, one local newspaper started a "Tramway Accident Column", which makes amusing reading nowadays. For instance, a tram collided with a horse-drawn trap, the driver of which complained of having his ribs bent. Another trap in a similar incident had its tyre ripped off, the horse's harness broken, and the driver's hat ruined. On the more serious side, a horse with a broken leg had to be put down; whilst at Manor Park, on the East Ham Tramways, a horse was electrocuted by a falling live overhead cable.

The second Ilford section with double track, from the "Rose & Crown" to Mill Road, was inspected on 27th May, along with the Ilford Lane line, by Col. Von Donop, and the tram service to the Roding Bridge commenced on 1st July 1903. The Ilford Hill line was something of a mystery, but the following appears to be the answer. The line from the Broadway to a stub terminal outside "The Rose and Crown" was opened on the 27th May 1903; a short extension of double track to a crossover at the Roding Bridge was opened on July 1st 1903; the new Roding Bridge replacing one built in 1779, was opened on 14th July 1903 while in due course the tram tracks were laid down and connected to those of East Ham. After the Board of Trade inspection the line was opened on the 1st of April 1905. The townsfolk had now accepted the tramway and its benefits, and took great interest in its workings. The drivers and conductors now received a pay rise of $\frac{1}{4}$d per hour, making their rates respectively $6\frac{1}{2}$d, and 6d per hour.

In late 1903 the Tramways Committee confirmed the purchase of a bicycle for the use of the Manager to enable him to get quickly to all parts of the system.

The attention of the Tramways Committee was drawn to the loss of revenue during wet weather, when passengers were reluctant to ride on the top decks. Some enquiries were made regarding fitting top covers on existing cars; and a trial cover of the Magrini type was ordered from Milnes, Voss & Co. Ltd., and fitted to car No. 9. Details of the Milnes Voss top cover was :-

Six feet four inches high;

Windows which could be raised in one operation, the cog-wheels to be covered by a neat guard to prevent accidents;

Trolley to be fixed to the roof;

Decency Board to have two neat wood strips instead of three, the distance apart being suitable to fix the existing advertisements;

The sides of the car to be painted blue lined with gold;

Brass plates to be fitted on the T-iron guides for windows, so as to give the car a better appearance when the windows were down.

At first, the trolleys remained fixed to the existing masts, which protruded through the roofs, while the order to paint the cars blue was rescinded.

The councillors and officials were invited to the depot on 5th September 1903, to inspect and ride in No. 9. One councillor described it as a "Thames house-boat on wheels". It was of a primitive standard compared with the covers that followed it in later years. It was the first cover in the London Metropolitan area and, because of its shape, became known locally as "Noah's Ark". The councillors and others mounted to the top deck. The Chairman, Councillor Burleigh asked everyone to smoke, "whether it be cigarette, cigar or pipe, as we wish to test the ventilation". The car went to Barkingside, then to Chadwell Heath and back to the Town Hall, where all the passengers alighted, and retired to the Chairman's Parlour where, to their delight, they discovered bottles of liquid refreshment and a box of cigars. In this mellow atmosphere they discussed their impressions of the ride, which were favourable; and a recommendation went forward to purchase a further nine covers. On the matter of the cigars and drinks, Councillor Burleigh said: "They help to soften the hardships of public life".

The top covers were fitted to cars numbered 1, 4, 10, 11, 12, 19, 20, 21 and 22; the cost being £71 for each cover. The enclosed part was immediately above the lower saloon, leaving the balconies exposed.

A delegation had visited Salford, Huddersfield and Hull; and their recommendation of the cover they saw in Hull, was acted upon. (Whilst in Hull, the delegation also saw the new crematorium).

On the first top cover, the returns showed £1 per day extra in takings on this car, and an 8% rise in electricity consumption, equal to 1s. 4d. per day.

The results of the first six months of operation were that 2,715,771 passengers were carried, paying £12,550.1.11. in fares. (An average of 1.11d per passenger).

A Town's Meeting was called at the Town Hall on 13th January 1904, to fulfill the statutory obligation in promoting a Bill in Parliament empowering the Council to construct further tramways, to be presented to the 1904 session. This was a very stormy event, and lasted three hours, the opposition being both formidable and noisy. In fact, one of the local poets was prompted to raise his pen to record the proceedings in verse :-

THE CHARGE OF THE ANTI-TRAM BRIGADE

Push and shove onward, all up the Town Hall steps
Rushed the six hundred. The great anti-tram brigade,
Oh, what a row they made. All up the steps
Rushed the six hundred.

Up the anti-tram brigade; was there a man dismayed;
Rather the Chairman knew, someone had blundered.
Their's not to reason why; their's not to make reply;
Their's but to "Boo" and cry "Rot", "Bogey", "Bunkum", "Rats";
The artful six hundred.

Burleigh in front of them, Bailey to the right of them;
Burke to the left of them, volleyed and thundered.
Stormed at with shout and yell, boldly they spoke and well;
Pity to waste their breath. All on the Town Hall floor
Groaned the six hundred.

Have the cars really paid, or will the profits fade ?
All the town wondered, on the charges made
By the stand still brigade, the noble six hundred.

R.H.R. (With apologies to Alfred Lord Tennyson).

From Mill Road, known as "Ilford Bridge", the tram service ran via Ilford Broadway and Ley Street, and passed the Depot into open country. The track on this line was single, with passing loops, and entered Horns village at the "Greengate" public house, which, at that time, was situated on the north side of Perrymans Farm Road. The track then became double, and then immediately was laid so close that no two cars could pass, opening out at the "Horns" public house. This section of track was officially known as "double-single"; then, reverting to single, wended its way down the hill over the Cranbrook, and up the other side. There was a gradient of one-in-thirteen for sixty six feet on this hill. At first the tram service ended at the main gate of Dr. Barnardo's Homes; the Board of Trade Inspector passed the remaining section to "The Chequers" about two months later, after modifications had been made to the track.

The Chadwell Heath service started from Ilford Broadway, and was double track except for a short section near "The Greyhound" public house at Chadwell Heath. On each side of Seven Kings Station, the road ran on an embankment, but after a few weeks of operation, the road subsided at this point, and had to be rebuilt, and the track relaid. The overhead was span wires, then centre poles from Cleveland Road to the Seven Kings Hotel, then bracket arms to Chadwell Heath.

Meanwhile, the Ilford Lane route was being constructed and was inspected by the Board of Trade on 27th May 1903, a service of cars commencing at once, even though the official permit did not arrive until June 4th. This line was built as single track with passing loops with all the overhead cables suspended from brackets fixed to side posts.

There were 18 cars available when the system opened, all open-topped, and built by Messrs. Hurst Nelson of Motherwell. Numbers 1-12 had four wheels, and known as single truck. Car Nos. 13-18 had eight wheels, and were known either as double truck or bogie cars. Nos. 1-12 had fifty seven seats; Nos. 13-18 had sixty nine. All cars were painted in crimson-lake and cream, with maroon underframes and trucks. The side panels were decorated with the Essex County Coat of Arms, with side titles and fleet numbers in gold and shaded blue.

Among the refinements fitted to the cars were curtains and rugs on the lower deck, but it soon became apparent that these items were troublesome to keep clean, and were shortly removed. However, one set of curtains and rugs were kept at the Depot, and the curtain fixtures were left in Car No. 5, which, from then on, was earmarked for private hire work, when, of course, the curtains and rugs were placed in position.

*

THE SYSTEM SETTLES DOWN

To cut down terminal time, the Ilford Lane and Chadwell Heath routes were joined up, but this was not altogether satisfactory, as it caused bunching of cars, due to the single track in Ilford Lane against the double track in the High Road; so the Council decided to double the Ilford Lane line, as and when the opportunity occurred.

The new tramway service was immediately popular, and four more single-truck cars were ordered from Messrs. Hurst Nelson. These were similar to the original twelve, except that they were fitted with wire mesh round the top deck, instead of the elaborate scrollwork, which, due to the antics of children, was regarded as dangerous. These cars were numbered 19-22. Further items of equipment obtained for the necessary smooth running of the tramways were a horse-drawn tower wagon for attending to cables, from Messrs. Blackwell's for £75, together with a set of tools for use with the same, at £12.18.0., and a combined rail and sweeping car from the British Electric Car Company. This ran on bogies, had a water tank capable of holding 1800 gallons of water, and was painted in a pleasing livery of chocolate, lined out in white and yellow, with gold lettering. Sometime during 1915, a coat of Ilford green was applied, and lasted until the vehicle was broken up in 1937.

The iron scrollwork around the top decks of the original cars was now replaced by wire netting at a cost of £1.10.6. per car, plus 12/6 for fixing same. The Council was now showing concern for the top deck traveller in bad weather, a deputation visiting Salford, Huddersfield and Hull, to see covered top cars at work, as has already been described in Chapter 1.

In the meantime, the widening and rebuilding of the bridge over the River Roding was undertaken by Messrs. Anthony Fasey & Son of Leytonstone. The northern side was built first and opened to the public; then the southern part was demolished and rebuilt to complete the bridge in 1905. Tram tracks were laid over the bridge and connected to the existing East Ham Council line in Romford Road at the boundary. This line had been the subject of negotiation between Ilford and East Ham Councils, because a terminal at this point would have been useless to both authorities. As the East Ham service had been operating only from Manor Park, a suggestion was put forward that East Ham provide three cars, and Ilford one car for the Ilford to Manor Park service. However, an agreement was reached on 20th March 1905 that, for a period of seven years, East Ham Council would pay Ilford 6d. per car-mile for the use of the line.

The new bridge and line were inspected by Lt.Col.Druitt on 1st April 1905 and the service started shortly afterwards. The agreement between the two Councils was subject to review if the service was extended beyond Manor Park. The Ilford service to Barkingside was cut back to Ilford Broadway.

During my acquaintance with Ilford tramways, I saw Ilford trams on the East Ham section on two occasions, both in the middle 1920s. The first was whilst the permanent way car was unloading materials for track repairs by the Skating Rink, and, as an LCC car was following, it was compelled to cross the East Ham boundary, and use the cross-over outside the Coliseum Cinema to return to Ley Street. The second time occurred when Ilford Car No.23 went to the assistance of a West Ham bogie which became derailed outside "The Red Lion" public house.

In 1905, a five month census was taken to compare the takings of an open-top car with those of a covered-top car. Takings from Car No.1. (covered top) totalled £382.14.8½., giving a return of 8.60d per mile; while Car No.2. (open top) had takings of £330.13.11½d., a return of 6.28d per mile. Bearing this in mind, the Council ordered a further six top covers from the Brush Engineering Company of Loughborough. In these, the covers extended over the balconies, which were not enclosed. The roofs were dome-shaped. The cars fitted with these new type covers were Nos. 2, 3, 5, 6, 7 and 8.

In May 1906, Mr. R.G. Spurr resigned, and his place was taken temporarily by Mr. A.H. Shaw, the Council Electrical Engineer, who was expected to give a third of his time to the tramways, and the balance to the Electricity Department.

Trouble was being experienced with the bogie cars as they were apt to derail at points. These vehicles were of the maximum traction type, that is, the pivot pin of the bogie was set off-centre, so that maximum weight was transmitted to the driving wheels.

In an attempt to cure the trouble, one car had its pony wheels removed and replaced by ordinary sized wheels. However, when it left the double track at Chadwell Heath, it jumped the points, ran across the road, and demolished a coffee stall. The Board of Trade recognised the troubles that the Tramways Department were experiencing, but requested that they refrain from further experiment.

Barking Council were now also building tramways, but, due to certain physical obstacles in the town, could not connect them at once. A line from Loxford Bridge, via Fanshawe Avenue to Longbridge Road, and close to Barking Station, was leased to Ilford, whose cars commenced to run through on 7th June 1905. The agreement governing this working could be terminated upon either party giving three months notice of intention to withdraw.

The Council were happy with the encouraging start made by the system in 1903, and the following extensions were envisaged in the Ilford Urban District Council Tramways Act of 1904 :-

No.1.	Ilford Station to Barkingside Police Station via Cranbrook Road:	2 miles 28.75 chains.
No.1a.	Curve from Cranbrook Road to Ley Street:	1.50 chains.
No.1b.	Curve from Tanners Lane to Cranbrook Road:	1.10 chains.
No.2.	From "The Chequers" Barkingside to Tomswood Hill:	39.10 chains.
No.3.	York Road (Cranbrook Road) via Belgrave Road to Wanstead Park at Highlands Gardens:	78.60 chains.

No. 3a.	An East to North junction at York Road:	
No. 4.	Wanstead Park to the Redbridge, via a new road to be constructed:	76.40 chains.
No. 5.	Ilford High Road, via Green Lane to Bennets Castle Lane:	2 miles 00.00 chains.
No. 5a.	An East-to-South junction at High Road/ Green Lane:	1.35 chains.
No. 6.	Green Lane via Sunnyside Road and Loxford Lane to Ilford Lane:	1 mile 23.00 chains.
No. 6a.	An East-to-South junction at Green Lane and Sunnyside Road:	1.14 chains.
No. 6b.	An East-to-North junction at Loxford Lane and Ilford Lane:	1.14 chains.
No. 7.	Seven Kings Station via Cameron Road and Benton Road to Ley Street:	55.48 chains.
No. 7a.	An East-to-North junction from Benton Road Ley Street:	0.90 chains.
No. 7b.	A North-to-South junction from Cameron Road into the High Road:	1.00 chains.
No. 8.	From Cameron Road along Aldborough Road to St. Peter's Church:	1 mile 31.97 chains.
No. 8a.	A West-to-North junction from Benton Road to Aldborough Road:	2.50 chains.
No. 9.	Green Lane via Goodmayes Road and Barley Lane, to Little Heath:	1 mile 27.57 chains.
No. 9a.	A North-to-East junction at Goodmayes Road and Green Lane:	1.20 chains.
No. 9b.	A South-to-East junction into Depot by Kinfauns Road:	0.65 chains.
No. 9c.	A North-to-East junction into Depot by Kinfauns Road:	0.65 chains.
No. 9d.	A West-to-South junction at High Road and Barley Lane:	1.25 chains.
No. 9e.	A South-to-East junction at High Road and Barley Lane:	1.10 chains.
No. 9f.	An East-to-North junction at High Road and Barley Lane:	1.40 chains.
No. 9g.	A West-to-North junction at High Road and Barley Lane:	1.70 chains.

A depot at Goodmayes was proposed as part of this expansion, with an additional one to be situated at the junction of Sunnyside Road and Kingston Road. The distance involved in these proposals was 11 miles 65 chains. Of this, only 2 miles 65 chains of single, and 3 miles 30 chains of double track were authorised by the Act.

A further Act was promoted in 1907 when proposals for three more lines were made:-

No. 1.	From Ilford Station to the Bandstand gate in Cranbrook Road:	
No. 1a.	An East-to-North junction from Ley Street to Cranbrook Road:	

No. 2.   From the Bandstand gate along Cranbrook Road to
          a terminus just past Beehive Lane, at the foot of
          Gants Hill:

The total length of these extensions would have been 1 mile 15.60 chains, but none were ever built.

The 1907 proposals only got to the planning stage. As the district through which it would run was "high class, residential", and in order not to offend the residents with unsightly overhead fixtures, it was agreed to explore the possibilities of equipping the line with the Dolter surface-contact method of power transmission.

As reference has been made to the surface-contact system, the demonstration track that existed from 1903 to 1908, at the rear of No. 49 Wanstead Park Road, will now be described.

This was the residence of Mr. Edmond Izod, the manager of the Griffiths-Bedell Company, the makers of the equipment. The line was one-fifth of a mile in circumference, and had a gradient of 1 in 32, and the curve radius was 54 feet. The track was paved, the sections being of granite, wood and gravel, a depth of 19" being required to install the system.

The car used for demonstration was a double-deck, single-truck type, seating 54 passengers, having two 25 HP motors, with Dick Kerr controllers, and was said to have been surplus to the needs of the Liverpool and Prescott Light Railway Co., for whom it was built.

A delegation from the Ilford Council visited the site on 10th March 1906, and were informed that speeds comparable with those in the main road were attained.

The car was fitted with a current-collector or "skate", six feet in length, beneath its truck, and this, in turn, was energised by a battery charged by the car motors. Studs of cast iron, 10"x 2", were set in the road at intervals of six feet. These studs were connected by a spring mechanism to a live steel cable inside an earthenware pipe laid below the road surface. The skate depressed the stud, which contacted the live cable below, and after passing over, the magnetised skate left the stud isolated; the spring-loading mechanism then returned the stud to its surface position and became "dead". The material used for the stud-to-cable contract was carbon.

This ingenious method of power transmission to a moving vehicle was installed by the LCC from Bow Bridge to Whitechapel, commencing operations on 25th June 1908, but withdrawn, after a series of mishaps, on July 17th. A further test was made in 1909, but the Council decided to modify the road surface to enable the conduit system to be laid. However, it may be noted that the "G-B" system of surface contact was in operation in the City of Lincoln until 1920.

The level crossing at Barking Station was replaced by a bridge which would connect the two sections of the Barking system, and, on completion in June 1907, the Barking Council started a service from Loxford Bridge to Fisher Street, and gave the Ilford Council three months' notice to terminate the through route, which expired on 30th September 1907. Likewise, the Ilford service finished at Loxford Bridge.

During the next seven years there is evidence of only one car passing the boundary, that was when a "Special" car took a party of worshippers to Barking Parish Church from Goodmayes, for which, the Barking Council asked ½d per person per journey.

An assessment of the system was made in 1907. At that time it had 6.5 route miles and 10.5 miles of track. The following figures were produced regarding the estimated life of the various types of equipment :-

    (a). rails: 9 years.
    (b). cars: 14 years.
    (c). overhead: 23 years.
    (d). underground: 32 years.

In 1907 also, the cars on the Barkingside route were cut back to Ilford Station, but this alteration did not last long, and the service was restored.

On 3rd February 1908, a service of motor buses started to run from London termini to Seven Kings, and an emergency meeting of the tramways committee was called to study the situation. As a result of their deliberations, a crossover was installed at Goodmayes (Barley Lane), and alternate cars were turned back here, giving the effect of higher concentration of trams on the High Road and, at the same time, fares were reduced.

The first motor buses belonged to the Great Eastern, London and Suburban Omnibus Company; these were quickly followed by Vanguard and General vehicles. This invasion brought with it a spate of accidents and accusations of obstruction.

In March 1909, Mr. A. H. Shaw resigned as Manager of the Tramways Department, to concentrate on the Electricity undertaking, and for the next three years, the departmental heads made their reports to the committee. Mr. A. Woolstencroft, the Traffic Superintendent applied for the licences, and his name appeared on the cars. The Ilford Lane track was doubled in 1909, and in this year the headlamps were removed from the dashplates, and fitted to the canopy bends, which action brought a protest from the advertising contractor, as it involved him in an additional cash outlay.

Despite competition from the buses, there was a need for more cars, and a further four were ordered from the Brush Company. These had four wheels, and top covers. They cost £561. each, arriving early in 1910, and were numbered 23 to 26.

The Ilford Depot had four roads and, lacking adequate paint shop facilities, a further two roads were put in and covered over. The ends of the tracks were sectioned off, and became the paint shop, so that the complete shed now measured 190 feet by 30 feet.

Meanwhile, the East Ham Council had purchased the horse-tramway at Manor Park, electrified it, and from 10th March 1909 a service of East Ham and West Ham cars ran from Ilford to Bow Bridge. The LCC were equipping the line from Bow Bridge to Aldgate, and commenced negotiating for a through-running agreement to Ilford. At first Ilford Council were not happy at allowing the large LCC bogie cars on Ilford tracks, but finally consented, agreeing that all cars paid 6d per mile. Although it was to be a joint service, East Ham Council were still responsible for the Ilford Hill track. On 15th December 1909, an LCC bogie car made a trial trip to Ilford. The East Ham Engineer reported that a half-service of cars commenced running from Ilford to Aldgate on 11th May 1910. The full service became operational on 25th May 1910.

The report of the Works Superintendent for this period makes interesting reading. For example, on 4th January 1911 he states that a 6'-6" wheelbase truck built at the Depot was put under Car No. 9 and was running satisfactorily. On 5th May, Car No. 21 returned to the Depot with two truck fractures, and was fitted with the spare one. The fractured truck, after being repaired, was put under the water car; the water car bogies were placed under Car No. 16, and, running the driving wheels forward, were found to give very good results. The bogies from Car No. 16 were made up as a single truck, and fitted to Car No. 6. About this time the motormen requested the Council to take all bogie cars out of service.

The stairs on the bogie cars were of the broken, or double-flight type, the run of stairs being broken by a small landing. However, spiral stairs were fitted to Car No. 16 on 5th July, and approved by the police. By the 6th September, Car No. 17 had also been fitted with a spiral staircase, and the Council agreed to treat the remainder in a similar fashion. It was again mentioned that the bogies under Car No. 16 were giving satisfaction; and, as at that time Car No. 14 was receiving attention for sagging platform-bearers, the opportunity was taken to alter the body and reverse the bogies. This entailed altering the braking system. Later, all the bogies were similarly reversed. A new truck, built at the Depot, was fitted to Car No. 3, and a seven-foot wheelbase truck was ordered for Car No. 8, which was in the process of having its platforms lengthened to permit a front exit. However, on completion, it was inspected by the police, who forbade the use of the front entrance en route, but agreed to its use at terminals, where, owing to the layover time, it was not required. In 1912 Car No. 25 was fitted with side roller destination blinds, but it was felt that this was not helpful to passengers, and they were later removed.

These very informative reports ceased in 1912, when Mr. Lionel Edward Harvey was appointed Tramways Manager, he having held a similar post in South Shields. His reports were brief, and leaned heavily on the side of finance.

One item which had to be settled about this time, was the re-siting of the centre posts along the High Road, from Cleveland Road to the Seven Kings Hotel. These had been erected in 1902, and by 1912, with the growth of motor vehicles, had become a traffic hazard. The advisability of the use of centre poles in the High Road, had been challenged at the time of their erection. Details of two fatalities have come to light :-

    (1). in 1904, a lad ran out of Richmond Road pushing a barrow. A motor cyclist, travelling in the same direction, swerved to the offside to avoid him, and his machine hit a centre post. The rider was thrown and died of his injuries.

(2). on 22nd June 1906, when a furniture van returning to Stoke Newington pulled out to overtake a stationary vehicle, the offside wheel struck the kerb base of the centre pole. The driver was thrown from his seat on the top of the van, and the wheels passed over him. The Coroner felt that the van should have been fitted with a driver's safety belt, "similar to those in use on the London horse buses". He further suggested that the centre posts should be removed.

During the discussion on the future of these poles, Councillor Everett, whose knowledge of local affairs and Council work far outweighed his command of the spoken word, was heard to remark that "these postes must went". The Councillors sat rooted to their boots, but after a short interval, they agreed that "these postes must went", and went they did. Those from Cleveland Road to Seven Kings Station were replaced in 1913 and 1914 by side poles and span wires; and those from Seven Kings Station to the Hotel, in 1919.

The track in the High Road from Seven Kings to Goodmayes, was re-laid in 1912/13; but there was little interruption to service due to the use of an overland crossing which was hired from East Ham Council at 10/- per week. This device was a shallow set of points, spiked down to the road surface on top of an existing rail. The tramcar could mount the crossing and be diverted to an adjacent track being used for two-way traffic whilst the other track was being renewed.

The competing motor bus service that operated along the High Road, had several alterations made to its London terminal points over the years. Service 25, Victoria Station to Seven Kings appeared on 20th June 1912, shortly afterwards joined by service 93, Bow to Romford.

Ilford Lane attracted the motor bus in 1912 when service No.86 commenced to run on 6th May, from Barking, via Ilford Lane and Cranbrook Road, to Barkingside and Chigwell Row. A further service appeared in 1913, when service 51 terminated at the Broadway from West Hampstead. This later split to reach destinations at Barking and Barkingside.

It must be remembered that the tram service in Ilford Lane was at a disadvantage, due to the need to change cars at Loxford Bridge. However, the Barking Council tram service from Loxford Bridge to Poplar had been extended to Aldgate in 1912, but the results were not satisfactory to Barking. So Barking Council negotiated an agreement with Ilford, whereby Ilford had exclusive use of the Barking track through Fanshawe Avenue, Longbridge Road and East Street, to Barking Broadway. The Aldgate service was cut back to the Broadway on 1st June 1914, and from that day, Ilford tramcars were to be seen gliding past Barking Town Hall to Barking Broadway.

This cut-back of operations left Barking with surplus tramcars, and the latest acquisition, Barking Car No.10, barely two years old, was driven to Ilford Depot on July 8th 1914. This car, together with a spare armature and axle, cost £650. After the change of ownership titles, and the fixing of the new

Brush car No. 24 outside the Town Hall.

Water sprinkler/sweeper car as supplied on bogies.

Car No.24 at Barkingside terminus in 1936.
(L.A.Thomson collection)

London Transport car No.304 (ex-West Ham 77) at Ilford terminus after the had been cut back to allow the installation of traffic signals at the road junction.
(H.B.Priestley)

fleet No. - 27 - the car was put to work on July 17th. It was noticed that the paint was in far better condition than the red on Ilford cars, painted after the Barking green had been applied, and it was agreed on the grounds of economy, that the Ilford fleet should henceforth be painted green and cream. It is recorded that all cars had been so painted in 1915, but this did not include the two cars requisitioned by the War Office, which remained red until 1919.

With the service now running satisfactorily into Barking, the bus service was feeling the effects of competition, and was withdrawn on 15th June 1914. Due to shortages brought about by the war, route 93 was withdrawn from the High Road, leaving only service 25 operating. There was a slight cut-back of the tramway terminus at Barkingside in 1912; a motor cyclist was in collision with a tram at this point and received fatal injuries, resulting in the tram being re sited in Tanners Lane, and the loop, excess track and overhead cables removed.

In the need for greater mobility, an Edison battery electric tower wagon, costing £695. was purchased and delivered in January 1914. The vehicle was driven into the adjacent power station for its batteries to be charged. It had a quaint appearance, having a low windscreen, and a cover for the driver suspended from the tower. Later, a cab, built at the Depot, was fitted. The vehicle had the registration number: F-7781.

In 1915, the Coat of Arms of Essex was removed from the 4-wheeled cars, and replaced by a new Ilford device, which showed the Essex Shield, Seven Crowns (for Seven Kings), the Barking Abbey Gateway, and the Fairlop Oak. In 1926 this was replaced by the Coat of Arms of the Ilford Corporation, which is a shield depicting the Fairlop Oak, the Seven Crowns and the rippling waters of the River Roding. The shield is supported by a Forest Verderer and a Barking Abbess, with the usual heraldic trimmings. At its apex is a deer (another Forest connection), while the motto declares "IN UNITY PROGRESS".

Milnes Voss covered car No. 19 and new Brush car No. 3 seen outside Seven Kings Station.
(Hornby Picture)

THE GREAT WAR

War was declared on 4th August 1914, and the first impact on the Tramways Department was the call-up of reservists. It had been the policy of transport and public utility companies to recruit staff from ex-military personnel, because of their known reliability and punctuality.

Need for extra cars became acute in 1915, and Barking Council were approached regarding cars which they had for disposal. Barking No. 8 was delivered to Ilford Depot on 10th July 1915. It cost £460, and became Ilford No. 28 shortly after Barking Council had confirmed its sale.

It had been the practice to put open-top cars through the workshops in the winter months, when their absence from the streets caused little hardship. Car No. 13 entered in November 1915, and was painted green and cream. Before No. 14 could follow, an officer of the Royal Engineers arrived at the Depot with papers authorising the requisitioning of two bogie tramcars as mobile searchlight units, as part of a War Office plan to place two rings of searchlights around London to combat the zeppelin menace. The Depot staff carried out the conversions, which required all top deck seats to be removed; a standard 120 cm. light to be fitted at top-floor level at one end. The other side of the trolley mast was occupied by a sheet-steel shelter for the operatives. All lower deck windows were boarded up. Inside was a generator which took its power from the overhead line supply. The other end of the saloon was used for messing purposes. This was kept locked during the day, my informant told me, and said, "every day a food wagon called at the depot with rations for the Royal Engineers who operated the light, but every third day, an ammunition wagon turned up, and the soldiers would unlock, and enter the saloon. Because of this, we felt there was a gun on board, perhaps one of the Lewis variety".

Thus car No. 14 became the first searchlight. Meanwhile, Car No. 15 had been involved in an accident, and was stood aside; Car No. 16 becoming the second mobile searchlight. These cars took up their stations each night; one at Barkingside terminus, and the other at Chadwell Heath terminus, both outside the Police Stations, where telephonic communication was no problem.

As the tramway staff were not permitted to enter the saloons, all maintenance work was carried out from underneath the vehicles.

There was one such unit at Croydon, and six in the northern and western areas of London, these latter being driven by tramdrivers from South Shields and Tynemouth, enrolled in the Tyneside Engineers.

After the Ilford units had been at work for some time, a fault developed in one of the generators causing the light to dim out. The War Department sent a replacement, which was fitted, the faulty generator being left lying in the Depot. The officer-in-charge was tactfully approached as to its future, but he ventured to suggest that the War Office was too busy to worry about one faulty generator. So the tramway staff corrected the fault, and set it up and used it to charge the Edison Tower Wagon, which, up to then, had been charged at the adjacent electricity works. The other two generators were the subject of much hard bargaining between Ilford Council and the War Office when hostilities ceased. The Council offered £50; the War Office wanted £100. They finally settled for £75. They were fitted up in the Council's Works Depot, and used to charge the batteries of some "Orwell" dust wagons.

Before leaving the searchlights, I feel that it would not be out of place to record details of an experiment carried out by the War Department at Lambourne End during this time. It involved a large searchlight of 150cm., fitted with a gold-plated reflector, giving an amber beam. It was intended to pierce mist and low cloud. By flying an aeroplane above it, it was confirmed that penetration was made. Unfortunately, the human eye at ground level could not follow the beam through. (Perhaps the amber fog-lamps now in use by motorists, originated from this experiment).

After Cars Nos. 14 and 16 were handed back, they went through the shops and were painted green and cream. No. 16 was subsequently involved in a rather curious accident. It was running on bogies at the time, and met Car No. 1 on the double-single track in Horns Road. It limped back to the Depot with all four axles bent. The drivers were reported as being a part-time man and a recently discharged ex-service man.

Within a month of the war starting, nine men had joined the colours. The drain continued, and, in 1916, the first conductresses appeared on the cars and remained until the war finished and the men returned.

From 1916 onwards, certain machinery at the depot was utilised on munition work. Because of the manpower shortage, maintenance lagged, and as a child I witnessed an incident in which, luckily, no one was hurt. We lived in Ley Street, and outside the next house was a standard with a bracket-arm attached, holding the overhead cables. One summer evening I noticed that each tramcar that passed appeared to lift the bracket arm up; after the tram had passed, it fell back to its original position. It appeared that the standard had corroded half way up. Then a car passed under quite speedily, and the top of the standard broke off, complete with bracket-arm and, still being attached to the overhead cables, swung out into the road. In a matter of minutes, the Edison Tower Wagon was on the scene, and detached the overhead cables. The bracket-arm was then lowered and deposited in an alleyway until next day, when a new post was erected about two feet away from the broken one; the bracket-arm and its attachments being transferred to the new standard. The Department was not keen for a repeat performance, and made an inspection of the poles. Any that showed signs of corrosion had the knobs or finials removed from the tops; the posts were filled with concrete, and the finials replaced.

The Armistice took effect as from 11th November 1918. Slowly, things got back to normal, and, in July 1919, the Manager, Mr. L. E. Harvey, put forward a plan to operate a motor bus service. He envisaged two circular routes :-

(1). from York Road to Belgrave Road,
Stanhope Gardens, Clarendon Gardens,
(or Cowley Road), thence to Cranbrook Road,
back to York Road, Ilford;

(2). from Goodmayes Station via Goodmayes Road,
Green Lane, Seven Kings Road, Cameron Road,
Aldborough Road, Meands Lane, Westwood Road,
Athol Road and Barley Lane back to Goodmayes
Station.

He calculated using two buses in each direction on each service, and having two spares, making a total of ten in all. He further suggested that some of these buses could be used on Sundays for excursion trips. However, the Council did not approve of these proposals and no further plans were forthcoming, in which the Council appeared as a motor bus operator.

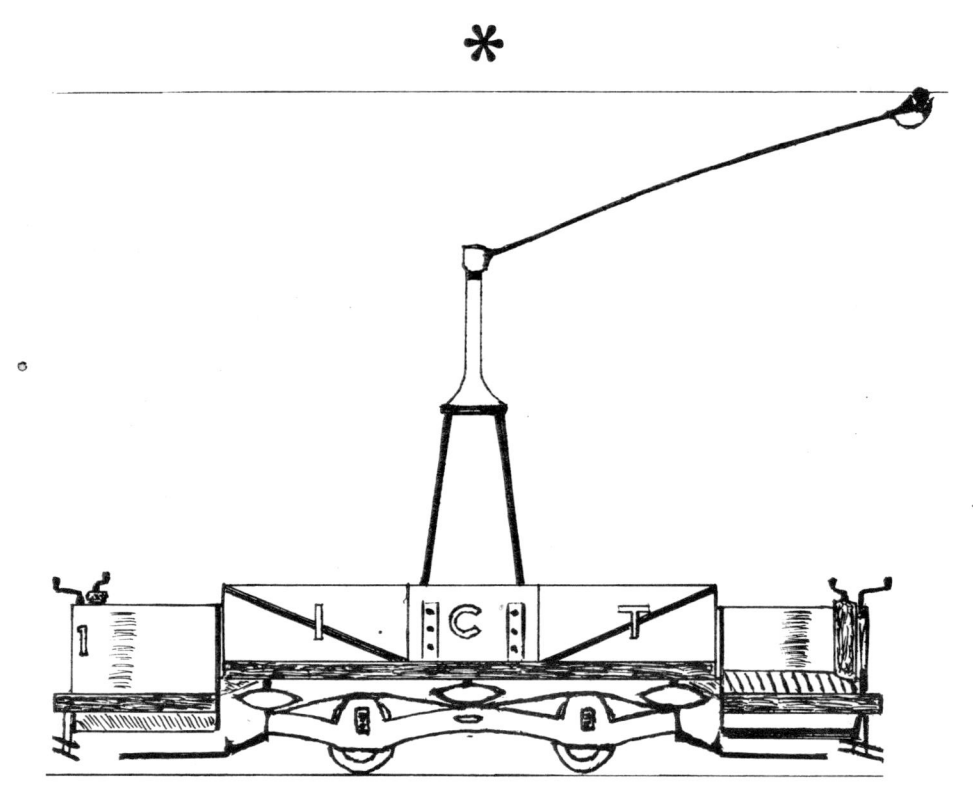

*

Permanent Way Car No.1 built from parts of Passenger Car No.1 in 1921
The trolley mast stood on a trestle made from angle iron.

ERO
after
LAT

THE TWENTIES

After the Armistice, things gradually returned to normal. To assist the backlog of maintenance, the Ilford Council ordered six new tramcars to be built by the Brush Company of Loughborough. These were similar to the 1909 batch, although seating 64 against 54 for the 1909 cars; they cost £2,016 each, and the first was delivered in September 1920, with the others following at intervals.

About this time there was a coal strike, and in order to conserve coal supplies, the tram service was cut back to Goodmayes in slack hours, Chadwell Heath being reached at peak periods only.

However, I feel I must tell the story of the top deck of No.4. I had started school in January 1920. After lunch break one day, with three of my young companions, we made our way down Ley Street towards Christchurch School, and became transfixed by what we saw standing outside the local cafe. Here was a steam traction engine, with, on its attached trailer, the top deck of the new tram No.4. This was longer than the trailer, and in consequence, overlapped it. On further investigation we found that, by bobbing under the balcony, and climbing on to the trailer, we could push ourselves around the balcony seats, which was accompanied by much laughter. "Quiet", said someone, "here comes the driver", who, with his mate, mounted the engine. Soon, we were off, and we waved to other children going to school. By this time the driver was aware that he had stowaways aboard, but he was very nice about it all, and stopping at Christchurch Road, he allowed us to get off. The top deck continued its journey to the Depot, where it was hoisted on to the waiting lower deck, and finally assembled before taking to the road. On reflection, I suppose that we could claim that we were of the few that had ridden on the top deck of a tram that had no lower deck, and one that was driven by steam instead of by electricity.

The new cars were allocated the fleet numbers 1 to 6, which meant a reshuffle in the fleet which occurred as follows :-

(a). the "Noah's Ark" type cars, Nos.4, 9 and 21, were broken up;
(b). No.1 received a truck body, and was used to convey materials to the site of track maintenance.

The top decks of these cars were placed in the Depot yard as store sheds.

(c). The domed-roofed cars No.2, 3, 5 and 6, were renumbered 20, 22, 21 and 9 respectively;
(c). the "Noah's Ark" type Nos.20 and 22, became 29 and 30.

One Saturday early in 1921 I noted that all the cars were sporting a white ribbon bow at the top of the hand rail at each end of the lower deck and, on asking the reason for this, was told that it marked the wedding day of one of the staff. Likewise, if I should see a black ribbon, this would signify the funeral day of a staff member.

About this time a new line was laid from the Ley Street track through a gap in the Depot wall, where it doubled, and ran the length of the existing shed. Shortly after, a corrugated iron roof and sides were fitted. This new shed was to assist in accommodating ten new cars similar to the vehicles received in 1920. The first arrived in April 1921.

One sunny April Sunday afternoon, on passing the Depot, I saw a new tramcar inside, fleet No.7. After a short time, an Inspector appeared, and drove it into Ley Street. In a minute or so, "Noah's Ark" No.10 pulled up behind it, bound for Barkingside, whereupon the passengers were invited to "change to the car in front". The Inspector made a short speech in which he hoped that the travellers would enjoy their ride on this brand new tramcar.

Old No.10 was taken into the Depot, its working days were over. One by one, the other nine new cars were assembled and put to work. They took the numbers 8 to 16, and this meant a further reshuffle which was undertaken in the following manner:-

    (a). the "Noah's Ark" cars Nos.10, 11, 12 and 19 were broken up;
    (b). the domed-roof cars Nos.7, 8 and 9, became Nos.17, 18 and 19;
    (c). the open-top bogie cars Nos.13 to 18 were renumbered 31 to 36.

In the early 1920's, considerable house building was taking place on the Valentines Park Estate, and in the Gaysham Avenue district. In order to bring in the materials, a standard gauge railway was constructed from Barkingside mineral sidings, crossing Horns Road just south of Chase Lane. (In fact, Horns Road, Chase Lane, and the single track railway, made an equilateral triangle). It then went through a shallow cutting, and, crossing the footpath that later became an extension of Hamilton Avenue, ended in the plant yard north of Eastern Avenue, near Ashurst Drive. A branch turned westwards, and crossed the Cranbrook Road near the present library to serve the city housing estate. Narrow gauge railways were laid to distribute along the streets. It should be noted that the Horns Road crossing crossed an established tramway route, and the Ministry of Transport not only specified the type of crossing, but also the methods by which it was to be operated.

As many as eight trains a day passed through, and the tramway staff were notified of the times. A man was sent from the Depot to act as a crossing keeper. The tram rail was single track at this point, and where it met the train rails had four slots cut in it. On the approach of a train, the keeper would remove four slices of tram rail from the slots, thus allowing the wagon rail flanges to pass smoothly, the slices being returned for the tramway traffic. The crossing lasted about three years, and fell into disuse when motor lorries became easily available.

Works Car No.1 proved its worth in conveying road materials, but created obstruction to the service during loading and unloading. It fell into disuse in 1924, when a Shelvoke & Drewry low-loader motor wagon was purchased.

The method of conveying rails was noisy, if not novel. Rails were usually 60 feet in length. One end was attached by chain to the rear of the Edison Tower Wagon and, at about two-thirds of its length, it was supported by a rail barrow. This device had cast-iron wheels fitted to an arched axle, from the centre of which was suspended a caliper tong grip. This was attached to the rail when the barrow tipped. On pulling the handle down, the rail was lifted, the handle was lashed to the rail, and 60 feet of rail went trundling over the cobbled streets to the site of its requirements.

In dealing with the increasing volume of motor traffic, the Clock Tower in Ilford Broadway was now proving a hazard, and a Council decision was taken to remove it to South Park. Following its removal, the tram tracks were relaid, cutting out the north-to-east and west-to-south connections, and adding a new double track from Station Approach to Ilford Lane, thus enabling a tram service to run from Barkingside to Barking. This service commenced on 4th February 1923.

About this time, open-top bogie car No.33 entered the workshops and reappeared much altered, having had balconies fitted at each end of the upper deck, which must have increased its seating capacity by at least eight. Its bogie trucks were removed, their pony wheels cut off, and the two frame ends welded together to form a single truck having a wheelbase of nine feet. At first, the original suspension was used, but this proved unsound, and a pair of volute springs were fitted to each end of the frame. These, in turn were superseded by semi-elliptic springs at each end, and one pair of "Parabo" volute springs in the centre of the frame.

No.34 then went through the works, and reappeared with the same modifications, except that the Brill 22E trucks, removed from the water car some years earlier, were, in turn made into a single truck. No.35 followed, and came out on a Burnley single truck. No.36 then received attention and was fitted with a lengthened Peckham P22 truck, obviously removed from the ex-Barking car, No.27.

It was about three years before the remaining two cars received the same treatment. They were also re-numbered, No.31 becoming 37, and No.32 becoming 38. As in the case of No.33, their Hurst Nelson bogies had an added side frame, and, with pony wheels removed, ran on single trucks of a nine foot wheelbase.

The Ilford trams used a very simple braking system, and the hand brake was used for normal service work. Should an emergency arise, the driver would throw his On/Off Key into reverse. Such an emergency occurred in fog on the morning of 23rd February 1920 on the single track in Fanshawe Avenue Barking, when cars Nos.25 and 26 collided head on. A further accident took place late in 1923, and it was during the enquiry as to the circumstances that HM Inspector stated that should any further accident occur, with the tram brakes being blamed, he would order all Ilford trams off the road until a more efficient brake be fitted. At this, the Manager pointed out that a further four cars were in an advanced state of construction, and it would be too late to amend the specifications. The Ministry Inspector said he would accept this as a statement of fact.

The new cars that followed were stated to be fitted with reconditioned equipment, and were identical to the previous batches, except that no head lamp was fitted, and they received the fleet numbers 17 to 20. The existing domed-roof cars carrying these numbers became 37 to 40.

The postal authorities were constantly aware of the housing development in the northern part of the town, and during 1924 an agreement was reached with the Tramway Committee to provide a late evening postal collection. This agreement took effect from 1st January 1925, the service commencing on 19th January. Two oblong postal boxes were made at the Tramway Depot, one in service, the other as stand-by in case of accident. The boxes were kept at Ilford Main Post Office, and a postman would hook one over the dashplate of the 9pm weekdays and 8.20pm Sunday departures from Ilford Broadway to Barkingside. Some forty minutes later, on return to the Broadway, they were removed from the tram and taken to the Post Office for emptying. As a precaution against theft, the boxes were padlocked with a chain round the brake spindle of the car. The service continued until about 1931, when the expansion of housing justified a Post Office van being used for general collection in the area. Needless to say, the boxes were painted Post-office Red.

From 1908 the tramways had motor bus competition along the High Road, and, from 1912-14, on the Ilford Lane route. However, by 1922, the London General Omnibus Company (LGOC), and its associates faced competition from the owners of "pirate buses", so-called because they chose to run their vehicles over the more lucrative routes, leaving the LGOC to provide the basic services on the less well patronised routes. Many of these "pirates" were one-bus enterprises, and some did not last long. Their activities were controlled however by the passing of the London Traffic Act of 1924, compelling their schedules to be submitted and approved. Even the LGOC agreed, as it relieved them of much wasteful competition. After this the "pirates" became respectable, and they were now referred to as "independents". One route, started by them, and numbered 256, had an adverse effect on the takings on the trams in Ilford Lane. This route ran from North Woolwich, via East Ham, Barking, Ilford Lane and Cranbrook Road to Gants Hill, every nine minutes. The following buses took up the service when it started operating on the afternoon of 14th April 1925 :-

Victory	(1 bus)
Essex	(1 bus)
Renown	(1 bus)
Essential	(1 bus)
Miller	(1 bus)
Britannia	(4 buses).

There were Saturday afternoon, and Sunday excursions to Barkingside, as Route 541B, and to Chigwell Row as Route 541A. However, it was not long before difficulties arose, as certain buses failed to maintain their schedules, and an order was issued for the services to be withdrawn after Easter Monday, 26th April 1926. It was reported that on 30th April that Pat (1 bus), Martin

(1 bus), and the Britannia vehicles were still running, but by October, it was confirmed that all had ceased to operate.

The Tramways Department had a scheme for pre-payment of fares. 13 tokens could be bought for 1/- valued at 1d each, or 26 at ½d. These tokens, in the form of brass discs, were handed to the conductor, who would issue a ticket to the value of the tokens tendered. The popularity of these tokens waned over the years, and their use was discontinued after 1st April 1926, although pre-paid tickets continued to be issued to schoolchildren attending centres for special education.

To signify support for the coal miners who had been locked out of their work on 1st May, a general stoppage of work was called for by the TUC as from Tuesday 4th May 1926. An unfinished section of track repairs in the High Road was soon completed by the voluntary efforts of two councillors, the town surveyor, some town hall clerks, and many passers by. A decision to return to work was taken on the morning of Wednesday 12th May, and there was excitement during that afternoon, when car No.18 came along the street. The two men on it stopped and cleared away the accumulated dirt from the blades of the points, and then proceeded to the next set. The Ilford trams were back at work the next day, Thursday 13th May. The buses returned on the 14th with the Seven Kings busmen voicing their disapproval at the trammens' return one day sooner, but agreed that it would be pointless to pursue the matter further.

The Ilford Urban District Council (UDC) had been seeking Borough status for some years, and this took effect from 1st October 1926. There were celebrations on Charter Day October 21st; all the tramcars were gaily decorated, and HRH the Duke of York (later to become King George VI) presented the town with its Charter of Incorporation.

In the twenties, the Ilford football ground was well patronised, and the trams moving the crowds were often to be seen with about ten standing on the rear platform, on the stairs, and, on occasion, even on the bumper. A friend who worked at the Depot, remarked that the car bodies sagged so much with these overloads that the heading surrounding the windows often sprang, and had to be refitted.

The trams continued to make a profit. Figures for the years ending March 31st are :-

1926:	£2,446
1927:	£4,999
1928:	£8,674

During these years a dog which apparently belonged to the Depot, was often to be seen riding on the platform with the driver, and, at times would wait at a "Stop" for a tram to come along, and would then jump on the driver's end.

The basic design of the Ilford tramcars had not changed for over twenty years, but many of the component parts were years ahead of their time, for example, in 1926 a car was fitted with tapered roller axle bearings, the free running given on these reduced its electricity consumption, and shortly all twenty post war cars were so fitted.

A second SD freighter was purchased (Registration Number VW 6623) in 1927. This was larger than the original vehicle of 1924 (Registration Number PU 1457).

A start was made late in 1927 on rebuilding the domed-roof cars. No. 32 was the first to enter the sheds. This was the front-exit car on 1912. It lost its front exit, and the tudor-arch windows on the lower deck, and re-appeared a much smarter vehicle, running on a truck built in the Ilford sheds. Three other cars with Ilford trucks were treated in a similar fashion, Nos. 22, 29 and 30. 1928 also witnessed the doubling of the track between "The Bell" and Wards Road in Ley Street, and about a year later a further loop was added in Horns Road by Princes Road.

There were 206 staff in March 1926, their functions being as follows:-

Manager:	1
Cashier:	1
Traffic Superintendent:	1
Works Superintendent:	1
Clerks:	8
Inspectors/Regulators:	5
Motormen:	53
Conductors:	56
Shed Workers:	47
Permanent Way Men:	29
Permanent Way Gangers:	2
Office Cleaners:	2

By 1929, the number had risen to 239.

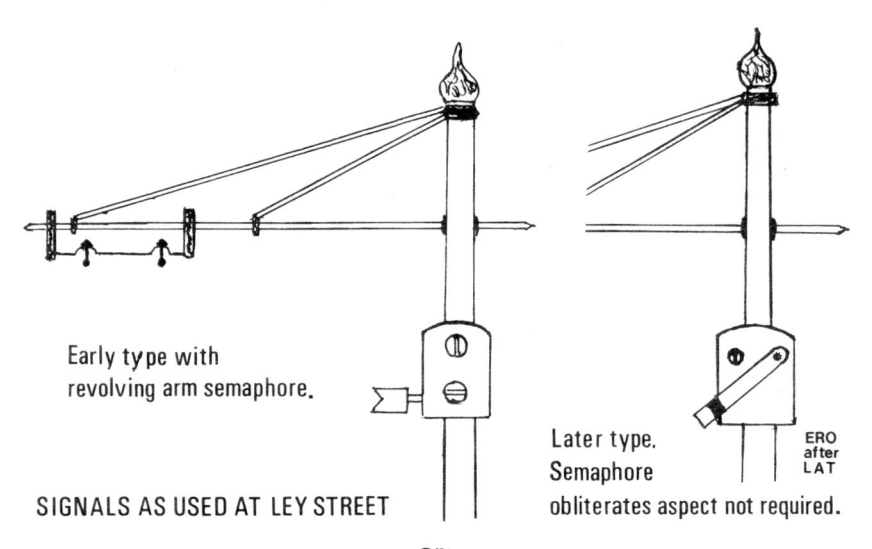

Early type with revolving arm semaphore.

Later type. Semaphore obliterates aspect not required.

ERO after LAT

SIGNALS AS USED AT LEY STREET

SCHEDULE OF
FARES AND STAGES

WHEN WORKING:—

Stages	Fare
BARKING BROADWAY AND KHARTOUM ROAD BARKING STATION AND HAMPTON ROAD LOXFORD BRIDGE AND ILFORD BROADWAY HAMPTON ROAD AND CONNAUGHT ROAD ILFORD BROADWAY & SEVEN KINGS STATION CONNAUGHT ROAD AND BARLEY LANE SEVEN KINGS STATION AND GROVE ROAD SEVEN KINGS HOTEL AND CHADWELL HEATH ILFORD BROADWAY AND PERTH ROAD HAINAULT STREET AND HORNS TAVERN PERTH ROAD AND BARKINGSIDE HAMPTON ROAD AND BELL INN	1D.
BARKING BROADWAY AND HAMPTON ROAD BARKING STATION AND ILFORD BROADWAY LOXFORD BRIDGE AND CONNAUGHT ROAD HAMPTON ROAD AND SEVEN KINGS STATION ILFORD BROADWAY AND BARLEY LANE CONNAUGHT ROAD AND GROVE ROAD SEVEN KINGS STATION AND CHADWELL HEATH ILFORD BROADWAY AND HORNS TAVERN HAINAULT STREET AND PRINCES ROAD BELL INN AND BARKINGSIDE LOXFORD BRIDGE AND BELL INN HAMPTON ROAD AND PERTH ROAD	1½D.
BARKING BROADWAY AND ILFORD BROADWAY BARKING STATION AND CONNAUGHT ROAD LOXFORD BRIDGE AND SEVEN KINGS STATION HAMPTON ROAD AND BARLEY LANE ILFORD BROADWAY AND GROVE ROAD CONNAUGHT ROAD AND CHADWELL HEATH ILFORD BROADWAY AND BARKINGSIDE BARKING STATION AND BELL INN LOXFORD BRIDGE AND PERTH ROAD HAMPTON ROAD & HORNS TAVERN	2D.
BARKING BROADWAY AND CONNAUGHT ROAD BARKING STATION AND SEVEN KINGS STATION LOXFORD BRIDGE AND BARLEY LANE HAMPTON ROAD AND GROVE ROAD ILFORD BROADWAY AND CHADWELL HEATH BARKING BROADWAY AND BELL INN BARKING STATION AND PERTH ROAD LOXFORD BRIDGE AND HORNS TAVERN HAMPTON ROAD AND BARKINGSIDE	2½D.
BARKING BROADWAY AND SEVEN KINGS STATION BARKING STATION AND BARLEY LANE LOXFORD BRIDGE AND GROVE ROAD HAMPTON ROAD AND CHADWELL HEATH BARKING BROADWAY & HORNS TAVERN LOXFORD BRIDGE AND BARKINGSIDE	3D.
BARKING BROADWAY AND BARLEY LANE BARKING STATION AND GROVE ROAD LOXFORD BRIDGE AND CHADWELL HEATH BARKING STATION AND BARKINGSIDE	3½D.
BARKING BROADWAY AND CHADWELL HEATH BARKING BROADWAY & BARKINGSIDE	4D.

WORKPEOPLE'S RETURN TICKETS are issued up to 7 a.m. for MALES and 8 a.m. for FEMALES at the following Fares :—

FOR ANY 1d. ORDINARY FARE AT 1d. RETURN.   FOR ANY 3d. ORDINARY FARE AT 3d. RETURN.
  " " 2d.   "   "   2d.   " " 4d.   "   "   4d.

PARCELS OTHER THAN PERSONAL LUGGAGE WHICH CAN BE CARRIED ON LAP OF PASSENGER, ONE PENNY PER PARCEL OR ARTICLE AT PASSENGER'S OWN RISK.

CHILDREN IN ARMS FREE, otherwise Children up to 14 years of age at the following Fares :—

FOR ANY 1d. ORDINARY FARE ½d.   FOR ANY 2½d. OR 3d. ORDINARY FARE 1½d.
  " " 1½d. or 2d. ORDINARY FARE 1d.   " " 3½d. or 4d.   "   "   2d.

TRAMWAYS OFFICES,
LEY STREET, ILFORD.

L. E. HARVEY, A.M.I.E.E., M.Inst.T.,
Manager and Engineer.

THE THIRTIES

The year 1930 showed no abatement in the construction of houses in the northern districts, and the Department decided to operate a peak hour shuttle service from Ilford to the "Horns" tavern at Newbury Park, and sought permission to purchase two additional cars to work the service. In fact, three bodies were bought from the Brush Company, costing £1,270 each. It was emphasised that the electrical equipment for these was "reconditioned" and not new, this being a neat way of by-passing the recommendations of the Ministry of Transport in 1924. These cars were numbered 21,22 and 23; the existing cars were re-numbered 41,39 and 40 in that order. No.41 did not last long, it being scrapped after about six months. Strange to relate, after this, the water car appeared with a domed roof, it having run for several years without any protection for the driver. Also during this period, a 9-foot wheelbase version of the now familiar Ilford truck was built, and fitted to open-top car No.34.

Some interesting equipment was purchased about this time to ease the problems of maintenance, including a tram-washing plant, a mobile welder, and a rail grinder. The welder and grinder took their current from the overhead wire, using an arm with a contact shoe which sat on the wire, thereby not obstructing the service. A new tower wagon was also purchased, mounted on a Vulcan petrol lorry costing £570. This vehicle had the Registration No. VX 9575, and was painted red all over.

The net profit for the year 1928-29 was £7,452. The other five East London tramway authorities each made a loss, and the following amounts were taken from the rates to balance the books:-

Barking:	£5,836
East Ham:	£15,900
Leyton:	£4,041
Walthamstow:	£39,655
West Ham:	£35,248.

Hence it was not surprising that Ilford Council lodged an objection when the plans were first publicised for the formation of an all-embracing passenger transport authority for London, under which, if it became law, Ilford would lose its tramway system, and the profits arising therefrom.

Advertising on the tramcars was in the hands of a contractor. All the adverts were fixed by the Depot staff, but were paid for by the contractor. A gentleman who held the contract in 1911 fell into disrepute as, although collecting his dues from the advertisers failed to pay the Department who terminated his contract. In later years, the contractor was a company, Messrs. Courtenay. Another source of advertising revenue was handled direct by the Department. This was on the backs of tickets. The Electricity Department, paid £100 per annum for an issue of between fifteen and sixteen millions.

Car No.1 appeared to be the subject of many experiments and, in late 1929, it received a set of toggle brakes of German origin. Although made mainly at the Brush Company's factory with some components from Dusseldorf, they were actually marketed by the Peckham Truck & Engineering Company. The type used at Ilford had two discs per axle, each twenty inches in diameter and eight inches apart, one being cast with the wheel. Each disc was served with two brake shoes lined with "Ferodo" material. Toggles operated the movement of the shoes to contact the discs, a 360lb. pull on the brake handle gave 17,600lbs on eight brake shoes, or 73lbs per square inch of brake surface. It was estimated that each car could go at least 30,000 miles before re-lining became necessary. (Cars used 48 blocks per year of the old type). Application was made easy at Ilford, as ball bearings were fitted to the hand-brake stem, and thrust bearings beneath the rachet wheel. Wheel tyres showed a saving by having no contact with the brake block, and having no grit trapped between wheel and brake block. Outlay was reckoned to be recovered in two to three years.

In 1930, the first steps were taken for the formation of the London Passenger Transport Board (LPTB), to which Ilford voiced its opposition at a hearing of the Joint Committee of both Houses of Parliament in July 1931. Mr. Lionel E. Harvey, the Manager, emphasised that the system worked efficiently, catered for local traffic, and had consistently made a profit to the benefit of the ratepayers. As will be seen, the opposition was of no avail.

In 1931, the Ilford Council agreed to the purchase of eight new cars at £2,122.5.0. each. These were to differ from the previous cars in that the upper decks were to be totally enclosed. They had large headlamps which held two bulbs; the steps were lower, and there was a step into the lower saloon. At the same time, six GE-200 motors were purchased from the West Ham Corporation for £300. Both these transactions were financed by a loan of £17,700 from the Ministry of Transport.

In May 1932, Barking Council requested that mens' Workman Return tickets be made available up to 8 am. By way of reply, the Ilford Council stated that they were greatly perturbed at the price which Barking Council were charging for the current consumed by Ilford cars on the Loxford Bridge/Barking route, which was 1.125d per unit, less 10% for prompt payment. For comparison, the following prices applied to traction current in other areas :-

Ilford:	0.90d per unit.
East Ham:	0.91d per unit.
West Ham:	0.875d per unit.

The negotiations ended in deadlock.

The new tramcars began to arrive in July 1932, and were numbered 33 to 40. They had the specified reconditioned electrical equipment, and toggle brakes. The eight cars scrapped on the arrival of the new ones were Nos. 28, 31 and the six op-top cars Nos. 33 to 38. Car 39 was re-numbered 31; and 40 became 28; the last two alterations being made to enable the new cars to

Ilford Corporation Brush car No19, built in 1924, seen at Barkingside in 1932.

(R.Elliott)

London Transport 31 (ex-Barking No.10) at Ilford Lane.

(L.A.Thomson collection)

London Transport cars 7 and 13 at the "Horns" tavern, both carrying notices announcing the impending substitution by trolleybuses.

(D.W.K.Jones)

No.43 stands at the Football Ground, Ley Street in 1937.

(D.W.K.Jones)

be kept in a series. The last car was licensed on 8th September 1932. The first one, No.33 had the legend "ILFORD CORPORATION TRAMWAYS", in large letters along the rocker panels on the sides. However, after about a month, they were removed, standardising the fleet in this respect. After a time, Nos.33-36 were to be seen on the High Road service, and Nos.37-40 on the Ley Street service. The nine-foot wheelbase truck built in 1930 for open-top car 34, was now fitted to the water car.

Time was running out for Ilford Tramways as an independent concern. The Bill was published on 13th March 1931, the Committee first sat on April 28th, but a change of government in the following October gave hope that it might be allowed to drop. However this was not to be. A White Paper was issued in July 1932, setting out the government's proposed alterations to the original Bill, which was given its Third Reading on 14th February 1933, the Royal Assent on 13th April, and the London Passenger Transport Act came into force on 1st July 1933.

The "A" Stock was equivalent to Debentures at $4\frac{1}{2}\%$ or 5%; The "B" Stock was a 5% Preference Share; and the "C" Stock represented Ordinary Shares, carrying a standard rate of interest of 5% for the first two years, and then $5\frac{1}{2}\%$ rising to a maximum of 6%. Most of the London tramway authorities opposed the Act because it lacked local control; but Ilford's opposition was based upon the Department's consistently profitable returns. The final consideration given was :-

£53,850	"A" Stock;
£53,850	"B" Stock; and
£53,850	"C" Stock.

On the passing of the Ilford tramways to the LPTB, the Manager, Mr. Lionel Edward Harvey, was offered a post with the Board's Technical Development Section. His later researches did much to make the carbon-insert trolley-head a success, especially with the coming of the trolleybuses. As to the tramways themselves, they became the responsibility of the Board's Eastern Area Tramways Manager, Mr.Theodore Eastway Thomas, who held the position until 1939, when Mr.S.R.Geary took over.

Car No.34, fitted with canopies, outside Seven Kings bus garage c.1924.

(Hornby Picture)

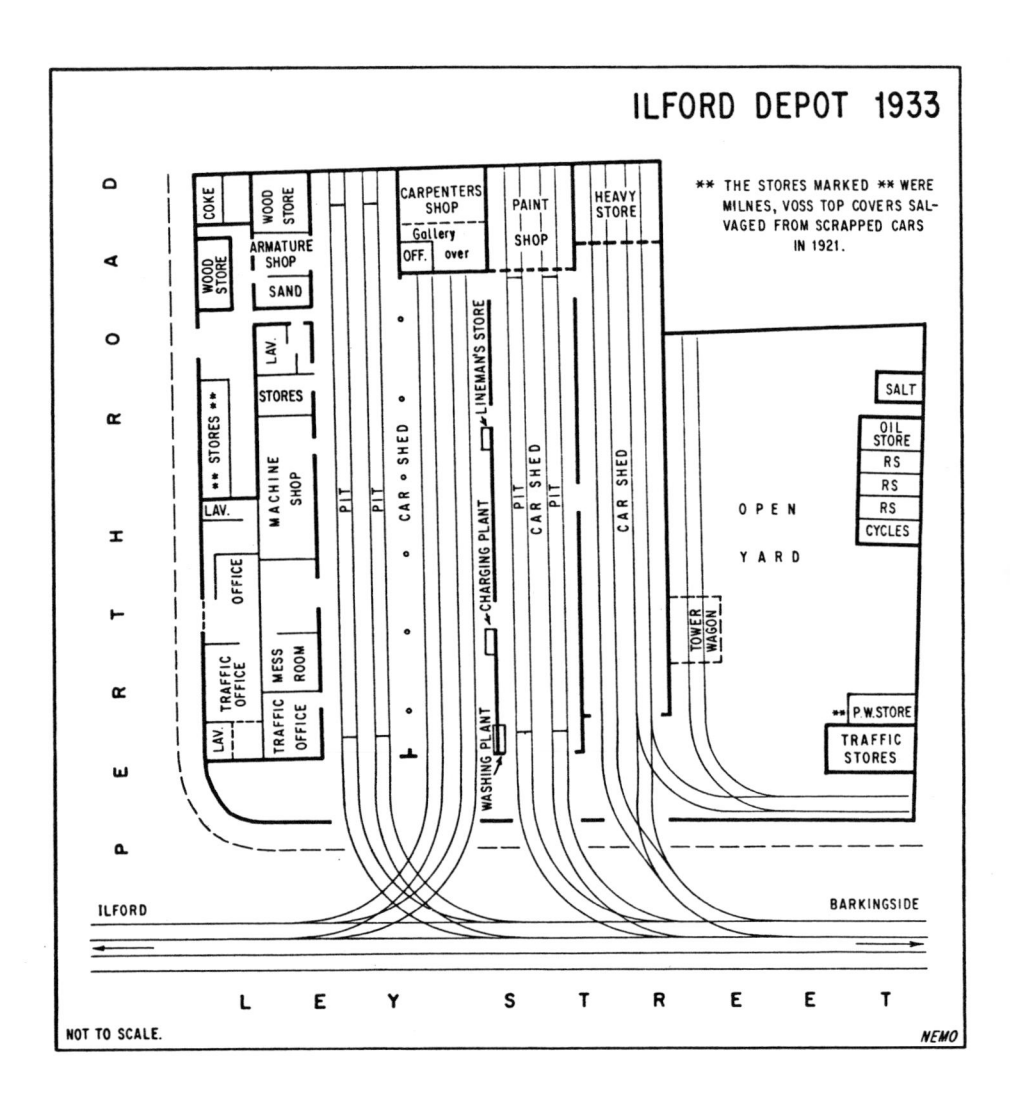

*

LONDON TRANSPORT

The cars appeared in service on Saturday 1st July, with slips of paper posted on the sides which proclaimed the new owners and their address at 55 Broadway, London, SW1. The local newspaper stated that the trams would shortly appear in all-red livery. The new car No.33 was in the paint shop at the time of the take-over, and emerged in the Ilford green and cream livery, but minus the coat of arms on the sides. The first car to be painted all red was No.2, and the second No.34.

With the merging of the tramcars under one control, and until such time as each vehicle had a different number, the ex-Ilford fleet carried the suffix letter "F" beside the old Ilford number. After about a month, the Ilford paintshop was closed, and the cars went to West Ham Depot for painting. I recollect seeing No.36 standing at Ilford Broadway with its front stove in; it would appear that the driver who brought it back from West Ham, was not acquainted with the Ilford brakes.

The numbering of the cars for LPTB was as follows:-

    Nos.   1-28   became 5 to 32.
             33-40   remained the same.
             29-32   became 41 to 44 (the domed roof cars).
           The water car became 057.

Within a year all the cars were repainted and renumbered. (The works car which carried the number 1, had been broken up about a year before the take-over).

The fate of the motor vehicles was different. The two SD vehicles vanished from the scene, joining the Board's Eastern Area Permanent Way Department. In fact, I saw VW 6623 at Bow, some time after. The Edison tower wagon, F 7781, had had its tower removed before take-over, and was used as a runabout, remaining in Ilford until at least 1936, and finally broken up still in its green and cream strip, and with the Ilford crest on the front. The Vulcan tower wagon was working in the Bexleyheath area, and was sold by the Board in 1949.

As it will have been noted, the Ilford tramway system had many customs, and also some equipment which was peculiar to itself, not shared by its other London counterparts. One such difference (and an important one too) was that its car wheels were turned to a profile that was different from the other London wheels, being cut from the flange downward and outward, as against upward and outward; the theory being that the rail would wear flat, and therefore last longer. On their own tracks, the Ilford cars were perfectly safe but, should they be used with such wheels on worn East London tracks, a derailment could result. On a bright Sunday morning in August 1933, London Transport sent an ex-West Ham bogie car to Barkingside, to test the theory that wheels of differing profiles could meet this problem. This one certainly did. The angled profiles of its wheels had little contact with the flat Ilford rails, and it only reached Barkingside after a lot of driving-wheel spin, and motors overheating. It was brought back to Ilford Depot and left for about four hours to cool down, and then returned to West Ham.

As yet, no mention has been made of fares collection. Ilford favoured Bell Punches, and this system was carried on by London Transport until the 1950s, in the days of the trolleybuses, when the Gibson ticket machine took over. The Bell Punch tickets issued by Ilford were:-

½d	brown:	1d	white;
1½d	buff:	2d	red;
2½d	blue:	3d	green;
3½d	yellow:	4d	orange;
	4½d	purple:	

As this last value covered the journey from Barking to Chadwell Heath only, it was later reduced to 4d. A grey, 1d Parcel ticket was issued to cover the conveyance of boxes of fish, that were stacked in the road at Ilford Station, and loaded on the Barkingside route on the front platforms of trams by fishmongers, who then rode on the tram to Barkingside and their own shops.

Workmen Returns were issued to the value of 1d, 2d, 3d and 4d, in the same colour as the single tickets. Such tickets were issued up to 7am for men, and 8am for women. The ½d pre-paid ticket was white with a vertical blue stripe, whilst the 1d pre-paid ticket was white with a red vertical stripe.

We now come to uniforms, which were originally blue serge with red piping. Overcoats were issued every two years, as also were summer and winter-weight tunics. Caps bore a brass script which stated the grade "Motorman" or "Conductor". About 1916, after the cars had changed their livery to green and cream, the uniforms became grey with green piping; and, in the 1920s, the cap band and epaulettes were of bright green material. Mr. J. C. Richards, the Chief Inspector, designed an oilskin coat in 1914 which was used by the Department. (It featured overlapping arm pieces, and an attached cape). The uniforms worn by conductresses during the 1914-18 war were khaki skirt and tunic with red piping, overcoat, and a soft hat. The LPTB uniforms for tram and trolleybus staff were navy blue with red piping, with the Board's motif in red and gold on the cap.

The water-car-cum-snow-plough remained in the Ilford green livery. I saw this vehicle passing through Manor Park in 1937, on its way to the scrap yard. At that time, the Board was clearing surplus plant and material from Ilford Depot, pending alterations for the accommodation of trolleybuses.

There were no alterations to the services operated, although on 4th October 1934, the Barkingside/Barking route was numbered 91, and the Barking/Chadwell Heath route became 93, co-inciding with the speeding up of the services. This was safely accomplished on the Ilford cars by the fitting of Westinghouse braking equipment, removed from ex-LCC tramcars, and the controller brake notches were coupled to the rheostatic brake.

After the closure of the Ilford paint shop, an additional tramcar was sent to Ilford to maintain the strength. This was an ex-West Ham Car (No.53), which appeared to spend its time on the Ley Street route in its West Ham colours. On re-painting, it became No.261.

Late one night in 1937, Car No.30 was being assisted to Ley Street Depot by an ex-LCC "Karrier" break-down lorry. It seemed that an axle had locked, for one was raised on a trolley which ran on the rails, with the lorry pushing. It frequently fell off and had to be lifted back again. I never saw No.30 in service after that. Cars Nos.41-44, went to the scrapyard about this time, with West Ham Depot supplying any extra cars. I noted the following cars working the Ilford routes (local) in December 1936, Nos.261,265,273,275,279 and 282, 33 cars were required to work the Ilford schedules, 13 on service 91 and 20 on service 93.

The first indication of the coming of the trolleybuses was the erection of the overhead standards in Ilford Lane, commencing from the Barking end. Some locals thought that they were to do with the coronation decorations, as they coincided. Meanwhile, London Transport were advertising for sale eight tramcars purchased by Ilford Corporation in 1932. Sunderland Corporation expressed interest, and car No.38 was sent as a sample. They agreed to purchase this car and also the seven others as they became available.

As the last day approached, the tramcars had notices fixed to their sides stating that on 6th February, trolleybuses would take over the service, and as the cars arrived at the Depot on their last journies, a Leyton or Walthamstow driver took over. The cars to be broken up went to Walthamstow, and those for Sunderland went to Leyton, where they were dismantled and put on a train at Mile End for Sunderland, where they served for another sixteen years. The last tram arrived at the Depot at 1am, three quarters of an hour late, in charge of Driver Knight, and Conductor Davison. This car was London Transport No.32, which had started its working days at Ilford in 1910 as No.23. There were about three hundred people at the Depot that night to see the last Ilford tramcar off on its journey to the breaker's yard at Walthamstow. A local wag wrote to the press appealing for all martyrs who suffered the Ilford trams to attend the following day (Sunday) at the Depot at 3pm, where a thanksgiving service would be held in front of the redundant tramcars. I cannot say any persons attended, but there were no trams, they had all left the night before.

And so ended the lõcal tram services, although of course, service 63 was still at work between Ilford and Aldgate, the cars being provided by Bow Depot.

Almost at once the Council set about replanning Ilford Broadway and installing traffic lights. The tram terminus was set back about fifty yards (in front of the "Red Lion"), and an additional loop was added to the single track which carried the service to this point. The trams carried on until 5th November 1939. There were no celebrations to cheer the very last tramcar to go down Ilford Hill, for the war had been with us since 3rd September and, with the prevailing black-out instructions, no form of after-dark jollification was encouraged. Besides, many folk were taken up with the prosecution of the war, dubbed, at this particular time, the "phoney war". Many of the cars used on this Ilford/

Aldgate route were not scrapped, but put to work in south London, whilst others were stored at Hampstead, to make good possible losses by enemy action.

*

Trolleybus No. 1735 of class SA2 seen in Hainault Street.

(L.A.Thomson collection)

Class SA3 trolleybus, No. 1753, seen in Ilford Lane.

(L.A.Thomson collection)

48

TROLLEYBUSES

It will not be out of place to record the operations of this hybrid vehicle in Ilford. Firstly, its source of energy was identical with that of the tramcar. Secondly, the legal requirements governing its running were similar. Furthermore, the local routes were the same, being:-

No. 691 from Barking Broadway, via Ilford Lane, Ilford Broadway Ley Street, Horns Road and with an extension along Barkingside High Street, terminating at the traffic roundabout at the "Fairlop Oak".

No. 693 from Barking Broadway, turned at Ilford Broadway along the High Road, via Seven Kings and Goodmayes to Chadwell Heath, turning via Station Road and Wangye Road.

Other turning circles were:-

at Barking, using the East Street, North Street and London Road one-way system;

at Ilford, from Ley Street, using Myrtle Road, Thorold Road and Balfour Road; and

at Newbury Park, using Buntingbridge Road and Birkbeck Road.

These services were daily as from 6th February 1938. An additional service, No. 692 worked Saturdays only, from Newbury Park to Chadwell Heath, commencing on 12th February 1938. It was not a success, and was withdrawn on 3rd December 1938.

The first trolleybus recorded as running through Ilford under its own power was seen on 25th January 1938. There was 32 trolleys at Ilford Depot to work these services, the fleet numbers being Nos. 572-603, with registration numbers DLY 572 to DLY 603. London Transport classified these as E1. The chassis were built by the Associated Equipment Co. (AEC), type 664T. Bodies were built by the Brush Company, and seated seventy persons. The controllers were by Metrovick, and the motors were by English Electric, Model 406A1.

The Ilford to Aldgate trams were replaced by trolleybuses from Bow Depot on 5th November 1939. These buses were generally of classes M1, N1 and N2, all seventy-seaters with AEC chassis, although one M1 unit was constructed with a Metropolitan-Cammell body. All had Metrovick 206A3 motors, and English Electric controllers. The fleet numbers were between 1380 and 1669, with corresponding registration numbers in the FXH series.

49

The first year of the war was notable for its lack of activity in the London area, apart from the manufacture of the implements of war. However, there were aerial skirmishes over the Home Counties. But the 7th September 1940 saw the start of a terrible onslaught, which was to last many months, during which London was the principal target. Many of its buildings were destroyed, and many people victims. The transport system lost many vehicles, and the motor bus section temporarily made up some loss by hiring buses from provincial operators. Eighteen trolleybuses were hired from Bournemouth Corporation. These maroon and primrose vehicles were allocated to Ilford Depot, releasing the familiar red trolleybuses to work in other parts of London.

The Bournemouth trolleys were built by the Sunbeam Company, type MS2. The bodies were by Park Royal Coachworks and the English Electric Company. The fleet numbers of the buses that arrived in December 1940 were :-

```
        72    -    75
        77    -    83
        85    -    87
        89
        117, 123 and 145.
```

Of these, the following returned to Bournemouth in November 1941 :-

74, 75, 80, 81, 83, 85, 86, 89 and 117.

The remaining nine saw service in Ilford until September 1942, when they went northwards to Newcastle-upon-Tyne for the remainder of the war, their numbers being :-

72, 73, 77, 78, 79, 82, 87, 123 and 145.

In Ilford, their operations were mainly confined to service 691 Barking/Barkingside.

An additional service was started on 29th October 1941, numbered 695. It ran from Bow Church to Chadwell Heath on weekdays only. The vehicles were originally supplied by Bow Depot, but from November 1948, Ilford Depot made an allocation to this service.

On November 1st 1941, the first of the SA type buses arrived at Ilford. There were forty-three in all, built for export to South Africa, but retained in this country owing to shipping difficulties. The fleet numbers were 1722 to 1764. 1722 was registered GGW-722. 1723 to 1764 were registered GLB-723 to 764. Class SA1 comprised 1722 to 1733, with chassis by Leyland, and GEC equipment; Class SA2 from 1734 to 1746, chassis by Leyland, and Metrovick equipment. These vehicles were built for service in Durban. Class SA3 was from 1747 to 1764, chassis by AEC, and English Electric Equipment. These were built for Johannesburg.

All these buses held seventy-two passengers. They were eight feet wide, six inches above the UK legal limit, so a special dispensation was granted to operate them in Ilford, where the local depot commitments kept them away from central London.

The SA type trolleybuses spent their working days at Ilford. Nos.1730/2/3 were withdrawn from service in March 1955, and were sold to a scrap dealer in Stratford-upon-Avon in May 1956. Nos.1722/4 were withdrawn in January 1958. Nos.1723/5/6/8/9 were withdrawn in January 1959; and the remainder in August 1959. Apart from the first three, all the others went to the scrap yard of George Cohen at Colindale.

There were two service alterations in the last year of trolley bus operations :- Service 695 was withdrawn on 6th January 1959, and replaced by an extension of route 663, which became Aldgate/Chadwell Heath on weekdays.

At the latter end of 1958 work commenced on the re-building and widening of Ilford station bridge. Hainault Street was wired for trolleybus working, thus enabling the Ilford station bridge to be used for one-way working, south-to-north. Hainault Street became one-way working north-to-south. The traffic flow remained this way until the bridge was completed. Balfour Road was being blanked off at this time to make traffic control easier by installation of traffic signals at Ley Street junction with Cranbrook Road. This work was delayed pending the withdrawal of the trolleybuses and the removal of the overhead cables.

The end of the trolleys came on 18th August 1959. After fifty-five years, electric passenger transport disappeared from the Ilford streets.

All three services were replaced by diesel buses. Route 663 was covered by extra workings on services 25 and 86. Trolley route 691 became 169, and route 693 became bus service 193.

The conversions did not require so much planning and equipment as that from trams to trolleybuses. There had been a strike of road service employees from 5th May to June 20th 1958, which resulted in a loss of passengers, and, in turn, to a cut-back of services. The spare buses were used to start the conversions.

Ilford depot was closed down, and became a store. Now, it stables vehicles belonging to the Cleansing Section of Redbridge Borough Council, and so the building returns to municipal use for the successor of the Council which originally built it.

✱

TECHNICAL DATA ON ILFORD'S TRAMCARS.

Car No.	Type of Car	Seats	Body Builder	Truck Type	Motors	Built	Wheelbase	Length	Height at Trolley Plank
1-12	Double-deck Open Top Reversed Stair	57	Hurst Nelson	HN Cantilever	GE-54	1903	6'- 0"	27'- 0"	9'-10½"
13-18	Double-deck Open Top Double-flight stair	69	"	HN Bogies	GE-54	1903	20'- 3" total	33'-10½"	9'-10½"
19-22	Double-deck Reversed stair	57	"	HN Cantilever	GE-54	1903	6'- 0"	27'- 0"	9'-10½"
23-26	Double-deck Covered top Balcony	54	Brush Eng.Co.	Brush 21E	GE-54	1910	7'- 6"	28'- 0"	16'- 1"
27	"	54	"	Peckham P22	GE-54	1912*	7'- 0"	28'- 0"	16'- 1"
28	"	54	"	Peckham Radial	GE-54	1911**	7'- 0"	28'- 0"	16'- 1"
1- 6	"	64	"	Peckham P22	GE-200	1920	8'- 0"	30'- 6"	16'- 1"
7-16	"	64	"	"	GE-200	1921	8'- 0"	30'- 6"	16'- 1"
17-20	"	64	"	"	GE-200	1924	8'- 0"	30'- 6"	16'- 1"
21-23	"	64	"	"	GE-200	1930	9'- 0"	30'- 6"	16'- 1"
33-40	"	68	"	"	GE-200	1932	8'- 6"	31'- 0"	16'- 1"
1	Water-car	–	British Electric	Brill 22E	GE-54	1903	10'- 6" total	24'- 0"	10'- 6"

NOTES: Controllers on all cars: BTH-K10.